Jeremiah Chaplin

The Memorial Hour

Jeremiah Chaplin

The Memorial Hour

ISBN/EAN: 9783742861801

Manufactured in Europe, USA, Canada, Australia, Japa

Cover: Foto ©ninafisch / pixelio.de

Manufactured and distributed by brebook publishing software (www.brebook.com)

Jeremiah Chaplin

The Memorial Hour

THE MEMORIAL HOUR;

OR,

The Lord's Supper,

IN ITS

RELATION TO DOCTRINE AND LIFE.

BY

JEREMIAH CHAPLIN, D. D.,
AUTHOR OF "THE EVENING OF LIFE," ETC.

BOSTON:
GOULD AND LINCOLN,
59 WASHINGTON STREET.
NEW YORK: SHELDON AND COMPANY.
CINCINNATI: GEORGE S. BLANCHARD.
1864.

Entered according to Act of Congress, in the year 1854, by
GOULD AND LINCOLN,
In the Clerk's Office of the District Court of the District of Massachusetts.

PREFACE.

THE design of this work is strictly devotional, — to deepen in the hearts of its readers, with the divine blessing, a sense of the value of the Memorial Ordinance, and thus to rescue this precious rite from that formal and superstitious observance on the one hand, and that careless and irreverent observance on the other, which are, alas! too common.

It is evident from the nature of the Supper and the circumstances of its appointment, that our Saviour intended it to hold an important relation to the Christian life, and it has been our endeavor, as best we could, to set forth its great lessons of love and loyalty.

This ordinance is not an obsolete institution, — useful only in the infancy of the church, — but is pertinent to the spiritual needs of believers in all times, even the most enlightened.

Never, "till HE come" in person,— He who sustains a relation so vital to our spiritual life,— can we afford to dispense with the quickening influence of this endearing memorial.

Certainly, in this age of skepticism, religious conflict, and prevailing worldliness, it is all-important that Christians cherish an abiding conviction of the Redeemer's presence, as a living Teacher, Guide, and Master, and that therefore they carefully regard this ordinance, whose language is, "This do in remembrance of me."

That our presentation of this grand theme may help to draw Christians nearer to their Lord and Saviour is our fervent prayer.

To His favor we commend, and to His ever-blessed Name we dedicate, this humble volume.

J. C.

CONTENTS.

CHAPTER I.

THE NATURE AND SIGNIFICANCE OF THE SUPPER — SELF-EXAMINATION — PREPARATION — POETRY, ... 15

CHAPTER II.

THE IMPORTANCE OF THE SUPPER — POETRY, ... 32

CHAPTER III.

ITS IMPORTANCE — THE CIRCUMSTANCES OF ITS INSTITUTION — ITS SECOND APPOINTMENT — POETRY, ... 41

CHAPTER IV.

ITS SIMPLICITY — CONTRAST WITH ROMANISM — POETRY, ... 51

CHAPTER V.

THE MANNER OF OBSERVANCE — SUPERSTITIOUS VIEWS — POETRY,..62

CHAPTER VI.

ITS OBSERVANCE — FEELINGS OF DIFFERENT CLASSES OF CHRISTIANS — THE RIGHT SPIRIT — THANKSGIVING — POETRY,......71

CHAPTER VII.

ITS OBSERVANCE — THE DOUBTING AND FEARFUL — ENCOURAGEMENT — EATING AND DRINKING UNWORTHILY — POETRY,.....82

CHAPTER VIII.

THE SUPPER A WITNESS AGAINST SIN — HUMILITY AND CONFESSION — POETRY,..97

CHAPTER IX.

THE DEATH OF CHRIST A CENTRAL FACT — ITS RELATION TO THE SEVERAL OFFICES OF CHRIST — POETRY,....................106

CHAPTER X.

CHRIST OUR LIFE — THE NATURE AND EFFECTS OF SPIRITUAL LIFE — PRESIDENT EDWARDS AND HIS WIFE — THE RELATION OF THE SUPPER TO THE CHRISTIAN LIFE — POETRY, ...123

CHAPTER XI.

CHRIST A SUFFERER — CONSOLATION FOR THE AFFLICTED — THE DISCIPLINE OF SORROW — FELLOWSHIP WITH CHRIST — THE DEATH OF CHRIST AS RELATED TO AFFLICTION, ...140

CHAPTER XII.

THE HISTORICAL CHRIST — CHRISTIANITY BASED UPON SUPERNATURAL FACTS — NOT IDEALISM — THE SUPPER A MONUMENT — PHILOSOPHY, THE TRUE AND THE FALSE — POETRY, ...169

CHAPTER XIII.

A PERSONAL CHRIST — EXPERIENCE OF PRESIDENT EDWARDS — STODDARD — DR. ARNOLD — ARTHUR HALLAM — THE RELATION OF THE SUPPER TO CHRIST'S PERSONALITY — POETRY, ...183

CHAPTER XIV.

THE SOCIAL ASPECT OF THE SUPPER — BROTHERLY LOVE — IMPROPER INFERENCE — DR. JUDSON — POETRY, ...199

CHAPTER XV.

THE RELATION OF THE SUPPER TO THE IMPENITENT — A SILENT SERMON — SILENT OBSERVANCE — MRS. BETHUNE, ...215

CHAPTER XVI.

CHRIST'S OBEDIENCE UNTO DEATH — LESSON OF CONSECRATION — THE MONK — DR. JUDSON — POETRY, ...226

CHAPTER XVII.

CHRISTIAN BENEVOLENCE — THE WORK OF THE CHURCH — NATURAL PHILANTHROPY — THE DEATH OF CHRIST AN ELEMENT OF POWER — DUTY TO THE OPPRESSED — POETRY, ...240

CHAPTER XVIII.

A SUMMARY — REMEMBER CHRIST — THE RELATION OF CHRISTIANITY, IN ITS PERSONAL CHRIST, TO ALL THE CIRCUMSTANCES AND CONDITIONS OF LIFE — ITS TEMPORAL AND ETERNAL BENEFITS — CHRIST EVERYWHERE — POETRY,..........................252

CHAPTER XIX.

THE PROPHETIC CHARACTER OF THE SUPPER — CHRIST'S SECOND COMING — HIS PERPETUAL PRESENCE — CONSOLATION TO THE CHURCH — CHRIST'S SECOND ADVENT TOO MUCH OVERLOOKED — POETRY,..269

AND as they were eating, Jesus took bread, and blessed it, and brake it, and gave it to his disciples, and said, Take, eat; this is my body. And he took the cup, and gave thanks, and gave it to them, saying, Drink ye all of it; for this is my blood of the new testament, which is shed for many for the remission of sins. But I say unto you, I will not drink henceforth of this fruit of the vine, until that day when I drink it new with you in my Father's kingdom.

And when they had sung an hymn, they went out unto the Mount of Olives. — MATTHEW XXVI. 26—30.

FOR I have received of the Lord that which I also delivered unto you, That the Lord Jesus, the same night in which he was betrayed, took bread; and when he had given thanks, he brake it, and said, Take, eat; this is my body, which is broken for you: this do in remembrance of me. After the same manner also he took the cup, when he had supped, saying, This cup is the new testament in my blood: this do ye, as oft as ye drink it, in remembrance of me. For as oft as ye eat this bread and drink this cup, ye do show the Lord's death till he come. Wherefore, whosoever shall eat this bread and drink this cup of the Lord, unworthily, shall be guilty of the body and blood of the Lord. But let a man so examine himself, and so let him eat of that bread and drink of that cup. For he that eateth and drinketh unworthily, eateth and drinketh damnation to himself, not discerning the Lord's body.—1 CORINTHIANS XI. 23—29.

THE MEMORIAL HOUR

CHAPTER I.

THE NATURE AND SIGNIFICANCE OF THE SUPPER — SELF-EXAMINATION — PREPARATION — POETRY.

"*The precious blood of Christ.*" — 1 Peter 1:19.

THIS ordinance is full of significance. *First.* It tells of CHRIST. "This do in remembrance of *me.*" This is its distinguishing feature. It is the Lord's Supper. It is the Lord's Table. The blessed image of Christ rises at once to view, as the One altogether lovely, the object of supreme love and veneration, to whom all hearts should turn, before whom every knee should bow, whether of man or angel. It directs the church to look away from all human teachers and masters and mediators and saviours to Christ alone. It proclaims his infinite and everlasting "preëminence."

Jesus,—Jesus! that is the name "above every name,"—the name to be remembered, to be treasured and enthroned in our heart of hearts.

> "Nor voice can sing, nor heart can frame,
> Nor can the memory find,
> A sweeter sound than thy blest name,
> O Saviour of mankind!"

For a mere man to have instituted such an ordinance and such a perpetual remembrance of his name and of his death, would have been consummate vanity or impiety, coveting an idolatrous adoration; but how fitting that he who was "God manifest in the flesh" should call his people to "honor the Son even as they honor the Father;" that through the world's long ages, his Bride should commemorate his death and wait with longing eyes for his coming. It is Jesus that the ransomed church adores, for in him dwells "all the fulness of the Godhead bodily," and he is her Saviour and Lord.

Second. It tells of Christ *in the hour of his greatest sorrow.* "Ye do show the *Lord's death.*" It bids us look upon and exhibit a weeping, suffering, dying Jesus! — the "Man of sorrows," — the scorn of men, — tormented by Satan, — forsaken by friends, — under the hidings of his Father's face, — treading the wine-press alone, — his "garments dyed" in blood, — Christ crucified! What an amazing spectacle!

Third. It tells of Christ in *the hour of his greatest love.* He is suffering, dying *for us,* — a *voluntary* sufferer, — bearing *our sins* in his own body upon the tree, enduring the chastisement of *our* peace, draining the cup of *our* woe, wrestling with the dreadful "curse" of *our* trangression, meeting and vanquishing *our* deadly foes, — saving the lost through a baptism of blood! He is dying for his enemies!

Oh, infinite love! It passeth knowledge!

Fourth. It tells of Christ as *ratifying in his blood the eternal covenant of grace.* "The cup is the new testament [covenant] in my blood." It declares the *fact* of redemption through his blood, and of that redemption as *perfect* and *certain* to all his disciples. It seals the bond. Christ is our surety. His dying for his sheep is the pledge of his undying affection. "I will never leave thee nor forsake thee." "Because I live, ye shall live also."

Fifth. It tells of Christ as *bidding his disciples to renew their covenant with him.*

At conversion, the believing soul covenants with Christ, as its Redeemer and Lord, to be his forever. It lays itself and its all upon his altar. This surrender to Christ is most eminently a free and voluntary act. "With the heart man believeth unto righteousness." "Thy people shall be willing in the day of thy power." Never does one act so freely as when, through grace, he receives the atonement and gives himself to Christ. He is drawn by the cords of love.

At the Table, in sight of the symbol of his shed blood, — the "blood of the everlasting covenant," the blood which tells the story of infinite love, — Christ would have his disciples, from time to time, renew their pledge of perpetual fealty and obedience, assume anew their obligations to serve and glorify him, to join hands with him afresh as their publicly acknowledged Saviour and Lord.

While he would reaffirm his covenant with them, to be their Redeemer, and to bring them off victorious, over every foe, he would, by this very means, by this reassurance of his own unchanging love, remind them of their solemn covenant with him, of the obligations into which they entered at conversion and baptism, and would have them reiterate their pledges of fidelity even unto death.

Sixth. It tells of Christ as *inviting his disciples to commune with him, to sup with him, while he sups with them, and thus receive the blessings involved in his death.*

" The solemn remembrance of Christ's sufferings is the leading idea in this holy ordinance, though the consciousness of communion with him is necessarily connected with it. And communion with Christ necessarily supposes his redeeming sufferings and their personal appropriation."[1] The cup of blessing which we bless, is it not the communion of the blood of Christ? The bread which we break, is it not the communion of the body of Christ?" It is the participation in the benefits of his death. And is not this, in the profoundest sense, communing with *Christ himself*,— a coming to him as Christ crucified yet risen, to receive from himself whatever blessing his death involves? Is it not communing with him as a Saviour, the nearest and dearest of friends?

And is not this itself the highest benefit of his death,—that we may have fellowship with Christ? Hence there is more implied here than covenant-

---

[1] Neander. *Planting and Training*, etc.

ing with Christ, — it is a *communing* with him; it is being on terms of sacred and tender intimacy, no longer as a servant, under a covenant of fidelity, but a brother of the Lord, and a son in his Father's house. It implies the utmost possible freedom, the liberty of supreme love, the unspeakable privileges of adoption. Christ here invites his disciples to lay aside the spirit of bondage, and to know the freedom of the sons of God. And this is also a " pledge of their constant communion with him, till that communion is consummated in his immediate presence."

Seventh. It tells of Christ as *the perpetual life of his disciples.* In him and by him they have spiritual and eternal life. From him comes its continual sustenance. "He that eateth me, even he shall live by me. This is that bread which came down from heaven." The repeated and regular participation of the Supper — of the bread and wine, which represent Christ himself — indicates our constant dependence on him, the continual renewal of our spiritual life in him. "Abide in me, and I in you. As the branch cannot bear fruit of itself, except it abide in the vine; no more can ye, except ye abide in me. I am the vine, ye are the branches; he that abideth in me, and I in him, the same bringeth forth much fruit: for without me ye can do nothing."

Eighth. It tells of Christ as *the bond of union between his disciples.* "For we being many are one bread [loaf] and one body; for we are all partakers of that one bread [loaf]." "Since," says Neander, "the Supper represents the communion of believers with Christ, a reference is at the same time involved to the communion founded upon it of believers with one another as members of the one body of Christ." "They form one body in view of their joint participation in Christ." "Ye are all one in Christ." By eating his flesh and drinking his blood, which they do spiritually at the Supper, Christians declare their oneness with him and with one another. What a strange, glorious brotherhood!

Ninth. It tells of Christ as *risen.* "Till I come" — "Do this in remembrance of me," — these imply his resurrection. We are not to remember and adore a dead but a living Christ.

Tenth. It tells of Christ as *coming again.* "Till I come." This prophecy the Supper perpetually utters. Every time we partake of the elements, we declare our belief and hope in Christ's second advent. In like manner as he departed, so shall he return.

To partake of the Supper is therefore the expression also of a desire for everlasting communion with Christ. "To be with Christ"— to enjoy his visible presence—" is far better."

Eleventh. It tells of Christ as, in the largest sense, "*The Truth.*" By testifying our faith in Christ's death and resurrection, as we do when we partake of the Supper, according to its true spirit, we also therein express our belief in all his claims, in whatsoever is included in his nature and his work as a divine Redeemer, a divine and infallible Teacher, Head over all things to the church. Christ predicted his own resurrection, and regarded it as the sanction and seal of all his professions, — the grand and conclusive authentication of his mission. He did rise. To that fact the apostles witnessed, and to that, through the Supper, we add our testimony. We believe that Christ is to "come." Therefore he has risen from the dead, and therefore he is what he declared himself to be, the Son of God, the Saviour of the world. "For to this end Christ both died and rose and revived, that he might be Lord both of the dead and the living."

Twelfth. It tells of Christ as *the "resurrection" of his people.* "I am the Resurrection and the Life." "For if we believe that Jesus died and rose again, even so them also which sleep in Jesus will God bring with him. For this we say unto you by the Word of the Lord, that we which are alive and remain unto the coming of the Lord shall not anticipate them which are asleep. For the Lord himself shall descend from heaven with a shout, with the voice of the archangel, and with the trump of God: and the dead in Christ shall rise first: then we which are alive and remain shall be caught up together with them in the clouds, to meet the Lord in the air; and so shall we ever be with the Lord." "But now is Christ risen from the dead, and become the first fruits of them that slept."

What a sermon is this ordinance, rich in all gospel truth, full of Christ, "the Way, the Truth, and the Life."

"But let a man *examine* himself, and so let him eat of that bread and drink of that cup."

The solemnity and significance of the ordinance demand due preparation for its worthy observance. Often, it is to be feared, the table of the Lord is approached in a thoughtless manner, or without due consideration of what such an act involves.

The Word of God enjoins *self-examination*. This should be faithful and particular. It should be made in connection with reading the Holy Scriptures, and with prayer for divine illumination and grace. For it is a solemn thing to partake of the emblems of the Redeemer's sufferings and death. Let each disciple ask himself, Why do I contemplate partaking of the Lord's Supper?

Is it from the force of habit?

Is it because its observance is a rule and custom of the church?

Is it because I am a professor of religion, and as such, it would be expected of me to be present at the Supper?

Or is it because I hear the voice of my Redeemer and Master, " Do this in remembrance of me?"

Does love to Christ, gratitude for his mercy, a regard for his authority and will, and a sense of my need of his forgiving and sanctifying grace, lead me to his Table?

Do I seek herein to draw near to Christ, to renew my fellowship and covenant with him, my surrender to Christ of soul and body and all that pertains to me, as not my own, but as bought with a price?

Do I feel penitence for sin, and am I ready to put away whatever Christ forbids?

Do I desire to be like Christ?

Do I trust alone for salvation in his atoning blood?

Do I have fellowship with my brethren, as joint-members with me of the body of Christ?

Am I ready to forgive as I hope to be forgiven?

Such examination should be honest and thorough, as in the sight of him who searches the heart. But it should never be made apart from the *cross*. The most searching analysis of conduct and motives should be in connection with the fact of redemption for the chief of sinners.

We should look to Christ to learn our sin and our salvation, — the disease and the remedy. A right view of Christ will melt our hearts to penitence, and reassure our hearts in his pardoning love.

Let us pray that we may approach the Lord's Table with humility, love, faith, joy.

It will be eminently well, as a means of preparation, to read over with care the Scriptures which describe the institution and observance of the Supper, in Matthew xxvi., Mark xiv., Luke xxii., 1 Corinthians x. 16-21, xi. 23-34; and also the whole account of the last days of Christ.

Specially appropriate also are the fourteenth, fifteenth, sixteenth, and seventeenth chapters of John's Gospel, comprising the addresses and prayer of Jesus, which appear to have been uttered immediately after the Supper, either at the table or "while all were standing in the attitude to depart," or perchance in part on the way to Gethsemane, but more likely all in that "upper room."[1]

With such appropriate reading, meditation, and prayer, we should look forward to the communion season with the deepest interest, as an important means of grace, as a help to faith, as the hand of Christ to draw us nearer to himself. Let us go to the Table *to find Christ*, "seeking him in the bread and wine, seeking him in the spoken word, seeking him in the prayer, seeking him until we find him; lest we return sadly to our homes, carrying from this feast only what we brought; lest we pause half-way between unbelief and faith, between life and death, between the crucifixion and

---

[1] Ellicott. *Life of Christ*, p. 295.

the resurrection, between Friday and Sunday; lest we go forth with the sad cry upon our lips of the still fearful and trembling Mary, 'They have taken away my Lord, and I know not where they have laid him.'"[1] Finding Christ, we can say with the poor Irish believer who had been rescued from popish darkness, when asked what were his feelings at the Lord's Table, "I felt that it was the marriage ceremony which united my soul to my Saviour forever."

An incident is related by a Moravian missionary of a Christian Greenlander, which illustrates the spirit with which we should approach the Supper, and which will ensure to us the endearing presence of the Saviour. It was communion Sabbath with the little church in that land of eternal snow. The services had ended, the disciples present having all partaken of the commemorative elements, when this man, clad in his furs, appeared in the church to take his seat at his Lord's table; and sad was he to find the service concluded.

On inquiry, it appeared that his intense desire to be present had kept him rowing hard all night upon the sea, but his utmost exertions had failed to bring him to the desired spot in season.

[1] Adolph Monod.

How pleasing to Christ must have been his toilsome rowing through the long, dark hours, while love nerved his arm and made him care not for the weariness and loneliness, if only he might unite in commemorating his Redeemer's sufferings with his fellow disciples!

Oh, had we the same tender and earnest appreciation of the ordinance, the same longing to commemorate the Saviour's love, the communion season would be to us one of rich profit, and we should exclaim, —

> How sweet and awful is the place,
> With Christ within the doors;
> While everlasting love displays
> The choicest of her stores!

This is the Memorial Hour, — the hour given to the memory of Him "who loved us and gave himself for us," who once was slain for us, but ever lives, our Intercessor and King, the great and good Being who is the Source of all present joy and the inspiration of all hope for the future.

May it be so truly a memorial hour that every coming hour shall be fragrant with the name of Jesus, that our entire life shall be a Christian life, imbued with his Spirit, and consecrated wholly to the objects which brought him from the throne to the cross.

Thou Holiest Love, whom most I love,
  Who art my longed-for bliss,
Whom tenderest pity erst did move
  To fathom woe and death's abyss;
Who once didst suffer for my good,
  And die my guilty debts to pay,
Thou Lamb of God, whose precious blood
  Can take the world's misdeeds away.

Thou Love, who didst such anguish bear
  Upon the mount of agony,
And yet with ceaseless, watchful care
  Dost yearn o'er us so tenderly;
Thou camest not thy will to seek,
  But all thy Father's will obey,
Bearing the cross in patience meek,
  That thou might'st take our curse away.

O Love, who with unflinching heart
  Enduredst all disgrace and shame!
O Love, who mid the keenest smart
  Of dying pangs wert still the same!
Who didst thy changeless virtue prove
  E'en with thy latest parting breath,

THE MEMORIAL HOUR.

And speakest words of gentlest love
   When soul and body sank in death;

O Love, through sorrows manifold,
   Hast thou betrothed me as a bride,
By ceaseless gifts, by love untold,
   Hast bound me ever to thy side.
Oh let the weary ache, the smart
   Of life's long tale of pain and loss,
Be gently stilled within my heart
   At thoughts of thee and of thy cross!

O Love, who gav'st thy life for me,
   And won me an eternal good
Through sorest anguish on the tree,
   I ever think upon thy blood;
I ever thank thy sacred wounds,
   Thou wounded Love, thou Holiest,
But most when life is near its bounds,
   And in thy bosom safe I rest.

O Love, who unto death hast grieved
   For this cold heart, unworthy thine,
Whom once the chill, dark grave received,
   I thank thee for that grief divine.
I give thee thanks that thou didst die
   To win eternal life for me,
To bring salvation from on high;
   Oh draw me up through love to thee!

                ANGELUS, 1667. *Lyra Germanica.*

PRAISES to Him whose love has given,
In Christ, his Son, the Life of heaven;
Who for our darkness gives us light,
And turns to day our deepest night.

Praises to Him, in grace who came
To bear our woe and sin and shame;
Who lived to die, who died to rise,
The God-accepted sacrifice.

   BONAR. *Hymns of Faith and Hope.*

HAIL, sovereign Love, that formed the plan
To save rebellious, ruined man!
Hail, matchless, free, eternal Grace,
That gave my soul a hiding-place!

CHAPTER II.

THE IMPORTANCE OF THE SUPPER — POETRY.

"This is my blood of the new testament, which is shed for many for the remission of sins. — Matt. 26 : 28."

CHRIST himself instituted this sacred festival. It bears the seal of his own authority as head of the church. So has it been accepted by the church of all ages, and not, as some would have it, a mere pleasing ceremony, well enough to be observed, even conceded to be positively beneficial, but still not authoritatively enjoined, like baptism.

To the loving heart, which waits not for positive command, but delights to follow in the Saviour's footsteps, regarding the slightest intimation of his will as law, it would seem to be enough that, as in baptism, so in the Supper, we have the example of Christ. But all the circumstances of the institution of the Supper, and, added to this, the uniform language of Scripture and practice of the primitive church, as well as the important bearing of this ordinance upon the development of the Christian life, prove that it comes to us with a divine sanction. The expression " Till I come," shows that the Saviour expected its perpetual observance. It was not the personal expression of the love and reverence of his immediate disciples,—a memorial established by them after his decease, and which we are at liberty to accept or neglect. Emphatically is it the *Lord's Supper;* for his own hands, so soon to be pierced, first broke the bread and poured out the wine; and his own blessed lips, so soon to drain the bitter cup of anguish, first pronounced the words of consecration and benediction. Knowing the vital connection between a remembrance of himself and especially of his death and holy living, and also the many temptations to forgetfulness, he most graciously founded this memorial service. " Do this in remembrance of me." Amid the cares and temptations of the world, this ordinance lifts up its sweet voice of warning and welcome, telling us of Him who " loved us and gave himself for us," of him who is our strength in weakness, our friend in all times of need, the author and perfecter of our spiritual life, our trust for present good and eternal glory, the object of supreme love and adoration. Who can say that he is raised above the necessity of this quickener and helper of his religious life? Not surely he who profoundly knows himself. It is impossible to estimate the disastrous influence upon the church of the obliteration of this memorial service.

If then its disuse or its negligent observance would be likely to seriously impair the piety of the church, is not this a demonstration of its divine authority and a call to all the disciples of Christ to honor it and protect it from perversion or neglect, so that it may stand "until he come," a monument of his tender love to his redeemed, and a means of preparation for the marriage supper of the Lamb?

However it may be undervalued in times of peace and quiet, and especially of religious declension, it has not been so in seasons of trial and persecution. Then Christian pilgrims felt most sensibly their need of Christ, and longed to get nearer to him, their only refuge. Could we have looked into those upper chambers, or those wild ravines and mountain caverns, where the hunted sheep of

Christ had fled for security from the bloody foe to worship God and partake unmolested of the emblems of their dear Redeemer's death; could we have seen them sitting together as one in Christ, and one in suffering for his sake, feeling that he was their all in all; and then have seen with what calm joy they went forth still to suffer, and, if need be, to die for him who had suffered and died for them, we should never have thought slightingly of the Lord's Supper.

Still further are we impressed with its importance when we call to mind the feelings with which the Saviour instituted it; for they had reference not only to the Jewish festival, but to the whole scene connected with it. "*With desire I have desired*—I have earnestly desired—to eat this passover with you before I suffer."

In no sense was it a happy accident that the Supper was instituted, an after-thought suggested by the paschal feast which it immediately succeeded. It was much more; it was the result of an earnest purpose.

The Saviour had a longing desire to celebrate the *Jewish Passover* with his disciples before his passion. He who was most intensely human as well as most truly divine, who was possessed of all human sympathies in the largest measure, wished to meet the beloved companions of his missionary labors once more in the flesh at the social board.

But all his joys were hallowed, and therefore he selected for this purpose a sacred festival. And the passover, of all the Jewish feasts, was the most strikingly appropriate, as commemorative of deliverance from death by a special act of grace, and by the blood of a lamb, which was typical of Jesus, the Lamb of God, whose blood cleanseth from all sin. It were fitting that Christ should suffer amid the scenes of the passover, thus giving to its long prophecy of himself a complete fulfilment; and therefore fitting also that the passover itself should be exalted into a Christian ordinance, commemorative of that fact,— no longer to announce a Saviour to come, but "Christ our passover" already "sacrificed for us," as our deliverer from the wrath of God.

We must therefore believe that he, before whose mind the whole plan of redemption lay spread in its comprehensive harmonies, and gradually unfolding itself as the substance took the place of the shadows, and the "mystery of godliness" issued into a clearer light from the types where it had been hidden for ages, had this chiefly in mind when he intensely desired to eat the passover with his disciples. He wished to institute the memorial of his death,— the Lord's Supper.

Everything is indeed easy and natural; the human element of Christ's character touchingly comes out in the fraternal gathering, and the Jewish festival readily passes over into the Christian rite; yet the scene reveals a deeper than mortal love and a profounder than human wisdom. It was the loaf and the cup already on the table at the passover, that Jesus set apart for the new ordinance of his church; but the two — the Jewish Passover and the Lord's Supper — are perfectly distinct, yet in spirit essentially one; and thus we see the beautiful unity as well as progressive character of the entire series of revelations of God's mercy to mankind.

Lamb of God, may I earnestly desire to commemorate thy death! Thou wert the true "passover sacrificed for us," procuring for us a great deliverance. When the blood of lambs would not avail to our redemption, as only typical of thine own most precious blood, thou didst, in the fulness of times, present thyself at the altar and lay thyself upon it, and there offer up thy life a ransom for us. To this sacrifice of thyself thou didst hasten with eager steps, in the infinite pity of thy heart. How can I ever cease to remember thee and thy bloody anguish? I would anticipate with lively gratitude the season of commemoration,— the memorial hour. Bless it to my eternal good. May it deepen my love to thee, and increase my zeal in thy service!

Jesus, thou joy of loving hearts!
  Thou Fount of life! thou Light of men!
From the best bliss that earth imparts
  We turn, unfilled, to thee again.

We taste thee, O thou Living Bread,
  And long to feast upon thee still;
We drink of thee, the Fountain-head,
  And thirst our souls from thee to fill.

Our restless spirits yearn for thee,
  Where'er our changeful lot is cast;
Glad when thy gracious smile we see,
  Blest when our faith can hold thee fast.

O Jesus, ever with us stay!
  Make all our moments calm and bright;
Chase the dark night of sin away,—
  Shed o'er the world thy holy light!

There is a dear and hallowed spot
　　Oft present to my eye;
By saints it ne'er can be forgot,—
　　That place is Calvary.

Oh, what a scene was there displayed
　　Of love and agony,
When our Redeemer bowed his head,
　　And died on Calvary!

When fainting under guilt's dread load,
　　Unto the cross I'll fly,
And trust the merit of that blood
　　Which flowed at Calvary.

Whene'er I feel temptation's power,
　　On Jesus I'll rely;
And, in the sharp conflicting hour
　　Repair to Calvary.

When seated at the feast of love,
　　Then will I fix mine eye
On him who intercedes above,
　　Who bled on Calvary.

When the dark hour of death, the last
　　Momentous hour draws nigh,
Then, with my dying eyes, I'll cast
　　A look on Calvary.

O Son of God, who camest from above
  To take my flesh, to bear my bitter cross,
Show me thy tears, thy tears of tender love,
  That I for thee may count all gain for loss;

That I may know thee, and by thee be known;
  That I may love thee, and may taste thy love;
That I may win thee, and in thee a crown;
  That I may rest and reign with thee above.

     BONAR. *Hymns of Faith and Hope.*

CHAPTER III.

ITS IMPORTANCE — THE CIRCUMSTANCES OF ITS INSTITUTION — ITS SECOND APPOINTMENT — POETRY.

"And being found in fashion as a man, he humbled himself and became obedient unto death, even the death of the cross."— Phil. 2 : 8.

THE deep place which this precious ordinance has in the Saviour's heart, and therefore should have in ours, appears also from a more careful survey of the circumstances under which it was instituted. These were indeed peculiar, solemn, amazing beyond comparison. The Lord of glory is about to die! to die under "the curse!" as the Lamb of God. The scenes of that fearful hour are full before the mind of the great Victim; he is now within its deepening shadows. The last night before his betrayal has come, when he shall be laid upon the altar of sacrifice. He is now with his faithful and beloved eleven, the traitor — the paschal supper being ended—having gone out[1] to do his work of blood.

Here, then, just this side of the garden and cross of agony, as it were on the border of that sea of anguish whose waves and billows were about to roll over him, and were even now sending up their murmurs into his ear, he spreads the table, and would thus forever consecrate it in the hearts of his followers. Ere he passes into the gloom and the conflict which he knew were so near and would be so terrible, he pauses to appoint this dear memorial of his death. He breaks the bread, knowing how soon his own body shall be broken and torn by cruel hands; he pours and gives the cup, knowing how soon his own blood shall be shed, and a bitterer cup than was ever mingled for human lips shall be pressed to his own, and drained to the dregs. Precious memorial! Olivet's garden brings its crimsoned garlands to lay them upon the consecrated elements, and Calvary casts over the scene its hallowed memories of a love which no terrors could extinguish. Never

---

[1] "The question rises, Did Judas leave before the institution of the Supper? The other evangelists make no mention of his departure; but what Matthew says, xxvi. 30, 31, and the fact that Judas does not until a later period (vs. 47) return again to the circle of the disciples, implies that he did."—*Tholuck, Com. on John.* So also *Ellicott.*

was there such a night as this, never such a day as that which followed it. The sun was to look down upon a scene such as he had never witnessed in the four thousand years of his shining, and was to hide his face; the earth was to tremble, and the graves to give up their dead.

That in the full anticipation of such personal suffering he should so regard the welfare of his people as to appoint it, proclaims his estimate of its value.

How dear it should be to us! A dying testimony is stamped with peculiar interest and worth. A memento from the hand of a dying friend is cherished most tenderly. When a beloved and venerated parent speaks to his children from the borders of eternity, as they gather around his bedside, with what interest do they listen to catch every syllable that falls from his lips, feeling that the treasured wisdom and love of years will be compressed into those farewell utterances. They are his *last* words, spoken within the shadows of another world, whispered back ere he takes his upward flight, as most worthy of remembrance.

Dearest Friend! elder Brother! dearer than father or mother, Saviour from the wrath to come, " Do this in remembrance of me," are *thy* farewell words, spoken not alone to the few that were with thee in the upper chamber, but to all thy disciples even till thy second coming. To *us*, while thou wast soon to sink into the arms of death,—and what a death!—thou didst say "Remember me!"

Thus did the Saviour institute the Supper. But to show how high an estimate he put upon it, and to rescue it from neglect or desecration, a *second* time did he give it to the church, with new sanctions, and new instructions as to its observance. After his ascension, as he looked down from the throne of glory to which he had been exalted, his heart still yearning over his flock in the wilderness, he calls their special attention to the Supper, and to the circumstances attending its original institution, through the apostle whom he had subsequently appointed. "*I have received*," wrote Paul to the Corinthians,—and it is as much to the whole church,—"*I have received of the Lord*, that which also I delivered unto you, that the Lord Jesus, the same night in which he was betrayed, took bread; and when he had given thanks he brake it, and said, 'Take, eat; this is my body,' which is broken for you: this do in remembrance of me.' After the same manner also he took the cup, when he had supped, saying, 'This cup is the new testament in my blood: this do ye, as oft as ye drink it, in remembrance of me. For as oft as ye eat this bread and drink this cup, ye do show the Lord's death till he come.'" This was by immediate revelation of Jesus Christ, a direct communication to the apostle, an express authentication of the Supper as an ordinance of the church. It was virtually a re-institution of this sacrament.

It was not only as "the *man* Christ Jesus," in his deep humiliation and about to be led forth as a lamb to the slaughter, that he deemed his death worthy of perpetual remembrance. As the *Lord of Glory*, passed forever beyond all suffering, exalted to the right hand of the Majesty on high, amid the joys and praises of heaven, he places his seal afresh upon this memorial of his death. From the Cross and from the Throne is there a voice saying, "Do this in remembrance of me."

Perhaps one reason for this explicit instruction regarding the Supper to Paul — preëminently apostle to the *Gentiles* — may have been to rescue it from being considered as in any sense a Jewish ordinance, and to make it known as entirely a *Christian* sacrament, given anew to the universal church.

The Saviour would also preserve the Supper in its original integrity and purity, free from desecrations and perversions. *As* it was "received" from the Lord, *as* it was "delivered" unto us, so must his disciples observe it, both as to the manner and the spirit; remembering that it is the *Lord's* Table, as instituted by him, as showing his death, as designed to be a remembrancer to us of Jesus, our Redeemer and Lord.

O Lord Jesus, suffer me never to forget that the Supper is thine own most precious ordinance, dear to thee even in thy glory. For my own sake, as a most needful memorial of my most needed Friend; and for thy sake, most holy and gracious Saviour, as a sweet witness of thy most glorious work, at which angels wonder, and to show my loyalty to thee, my King, Fountain of all authority in the church, that I may prove even my supreme regard for thy commandments and ordinances and example,— oh, help me to be a faithful and worthy participant.

O EVERLASTING Love,
   Well-spring of grace and peace,
Pour down thy fulness from above,
   Bid doubt and trouble cease!

O everlasting Rest,
   Lift off life's load of care!
Relieve, revive this burdened breast,
   And every sorrow bear.

Thou art in heaven our all,
   Our all on earth art thou;
Upon thy glorious name we call,—
   Lord Jesus, bless us now!

BONAR.

O SACRED brow! though unbelief
   Discovers not thy majesty,
Beneath that veil of shame and grief,
   Its glory still unchanged I see.
Thy visage, marred beyond compare,
   Yet beauteous to my eye appears;
Those features heaven's own image bear,
   Even though defiled with blood and tears.

Nor, through the unending heavenly day,
   However great its splendors are,
More glory will that face display
   Than now its pallid features wear.

Even there in beauty's own domain,
    The eye shall ne'er such beauty see;
Such glory as adorned thy train
    When going up to Calvary!

Ye angels, who with equal love
    The Father and the Son adore,
Fulfilling in the courts above
    Your ministry for evermore;
Ye mighty seraphs near his throne,
    Think ye the Incarnate Mystery
Has ever with such radiance shone,
    As on the hill of Calvary?

The work of sacrifice below
    There crowned the heaven-descended WORD!
The shame of Mary's Son is now
    The glory of the Son of God.
My name is Love, the Father said;
    Jesus replied, when from above
Descended, on the cross he bled,—
    I am thy Son; I too am Love!

And very God and Love is he,
    The God through whom our God gives grace,
The God we love, the God we see,
    Uniting God with Adam's race!
Where then is glory to be found?
    Here, here, upon this shameful tree,
Where heaven's own king, a victim bound,
    Is made a sacrifice for me.

For Love is highest excellence,
   The source of all the joys above;
'Tis stronger than Omnipotence,
   And Jesus' richest crown is Love.
How vain the honors men possess,
   The honors of the loftiest state!
And heaven and earth alike confess
   That Charity alone is great.

From the French of Vinet.

O LOVE of God, how strong and true!
Eternal and yet ever new,
Uncomprehended and unbought,
Beyond all knowledge and all thought.

O wide-embracing, wondrous love!
We read thee in the sky above,
We read thee in the earth below,
In seas that swell and streams that flow.

We read thee best in Him who came
To bear for us the cross of shame;
Sent by the Father from on high,
Our life to live, our death to die.

We read thee in the manger-bed
On which his infancy was laid;
And Nazareth that love reveals,
Nestling amid its lonely hills.

We read thee in the tears once shed
Over doomed Salem's guilty head,
In the cold tomb of Bethany,
And blood-drops of Gethsemane.

We read thy power to bless and save,
Even in the darkness of the grave;
Still more in resurrection light
We read the fulness of thy might.

O love of God, our shield and stay,
Through all the perils of our way;
Eternal Love, in thee we rest,
Forever safe, forever blest!

BONAR. *Hymns of Faith and Hope.*

CHAPTER IV.

ITS SIMPLICITY — CONTRAST WITH ROMANISM — POETRY.

"I am meek and lowly in heart." — Matt. 11 : 29.

How admirable the simplicity of this ordinance! how in keeping with the whole character and gospel of Christ!

The religion of Jesus is not a religion of the imagination or the senses. It indeed acknowledges them and appeals to them in their proper sphere; for it is a system for man with an intellectual and physical nature. It sanctifies and calls into exercise every part of our complex being, aiming to bring the whole man, — body, soul, and spirit, — under its blessed control, and making all conducive to his highest spiritual welfare.

The religion of Christ, therefore, gives no countenance to that exaggerated spiritualism which affects to transcend the external senses, and discards all historical beliefs, dwelling in a realm of sublimated idealism.

Although the most intensely spiritual of all religious systems, it is yet most intensely concrete and human, as addressing itself not to pure spirits, but to spirits incarnated, and which shall forever be embodied, though in a sense to which our existing material forms furnish but a very faint analogy. And thus it may be that, as our Saviour intimates, though without explanation, the Lord's Supper will in some sense be perpetuated in heaven. There is to be a "drinking anew in the kingdom of God." What a spectacle such a scene would be in heaven! Would not the angels look on and wonder?

But it is a striking proof of the divine origin of Christianity, that it ever holds the senses to their proper place of subordination, making them honorable yet humble servitors to the higher spirit that dwells within. And so also the imagination, that soaring intellectual faculty, is taught to chasten its aspirings and to regard itself as only the lowly handmaid of faith, helping faith to gaze with keener eye, and grasp with firmer hand, and comprehend with wider sweep, spiritual and eternal realities; yet itself to veil its face and bow with reverent mien before the invisible things of God, which faith discerns.

A system of religion which gives great prominence to the imagination and the senses cannot, therefore, be from God.

In striking contrast with all earth-born systems is Christianity, in all its parts, aspects, and influences. The evangelistic record of the life of Christ, and especially of its last days and of his passion,— how remarkably simple and reserved! There is no high-wrought description of the different incidents of that last wondrous scene, no artistic grouping of events, no studied projection into the foreground of the various stages of the machinery of the crucifixion, no startling dramatic touches for effect. A few artless strokes, and the scene is before us; but not so drawn as to make its chief appeal to the natural sensibilities, or to foster a mere sensuous or sentimental devotion.[1]

---

[1] "The mysteries of those hours of darkness, when with the sufferings of the agonized body mingled the sufferings of the sacred soul, the struggles with sinking nature, the accumulating pressure of the burden of a world's sin, the momently more and more embittered foretastings of that which was its wages and its penalty, the clinging desperation of the last assaults of Satan and his mustered hosts, the withdrawal and darkening of the Paternal presence,—mysteries such as these, so deep and so dread, it was not meet that even the tongues of apostles should be moved to speak of, or the pens of evangelists to record.

How different, this sacred and delicate reserve, from the practice of some of Christ's professed ministers in treating of the scenes of his passion. Their detailed and revolting exhibitions of physical torture offend the Christian taste that has been formed in the school of evangelists and apostles, and fail to reach the true end of preaching Christ crucified.

Romanism proves itself to be another gospel, in its " morbid tendency toward the contemplation of bodily pain, owing to the attribution of saving power to it;" and this, "like every other moral error, has been of fatal effect in art, leaving not altogether without the stain and blame of it, even the highest of the pure Romanist painters,"[1] whose

---

Nay, the very outward eye of man might now gaze no farther. All man might know was by the hearing of the ear. One loud cry revealed all, and more than all, that it is possible for our nature to conceive,— one loud cry of unfathomable woe and uttermost desolation, and yet, as even its very accents imply, of achieved and consummated victory."—*Ellicott, The Life of Christ.*

[1] " In the common and most catholic treatment of the subject [the crucifixion], the mind is either painfully directed to the bodily agony, coarsely expressed by outward anatomical signs, or else it is permitted to rest on that countenance inconceivable by man at any time, but chiefly so in this its consummated humiliation. In the first case, the representation is revolting; in the second, inefficient, false, and sometimes blasphemous. None even of the greatest religious painters have ever, so far as I know, succeeded here."— *Ruskin, Modern Painters*, Vol. II., p. 174.

works are also among the acknowledged religious influences of that corrupt church. This method of Romanism, so wide a contrast to the subdued and chaste simplicity of the inspired Word, this bringing out into bold relief the various aspects of bodily agony, this unseemly dwelling upon the external, the horrible, the painful, may awaken the natural sensibilities, and open the fountains of tears, but are not adapted to touch deep chords within the soul, nor to produce permanent impressions. There are tears, perhaps delicious tears, which are taken as certain proofs of piety, but it is a piety which weeps itself dry,— for the most part, a vain and delusive superstition, which cheats the soul with a show of Christ, while it keeps out of sight the true atoning Lamb, and the deep, invisible, unutterable, inexpressible sorrow of soul which formed the chief burden of his death-agony. To exaggerate the surroundings and external appearances of the scene at Golgotha is superficial and false; it hides from us that deeper view, to gain which the outward is only a help. It substitutes tears for penitence and feeling for faith. It shows too exclusively the human side of Christ, the *man* Christ Jesus, and fails to impress us with that transcendent spiritual Presence, surpassing all human capacity, which sighed and groaned with a mighty grief in which angels and even nature sympathized, but whose divine depths no *mortal* line can fathom. It was the incarnate God that suffered; and human eloquence and human art should modestly confess their utter weakness to portray the scene, and be content with that simplicity which ever characterizes the utterances of profound conviction and feeling.

In this view, how admirable the extreme simplicity of the Lord's Supper! Its tone of representation of the death of Christ is reserved and subdued, marked by an entire absence of every revolting feature, yet strikingly significant of suffering, even as of a cart pressed under the sheaves or of grapes crushed for the wine, keeping, however, in the background the mere physical element of the scene, and making prominent to the mind the great spiritual ideas of humiliation and sacrifice, of sorrow and love unbounded.

For a visible memorial of that death which made earth to shudder, Christ uses no costly and rare materials, he makes no startling appeal to the outward senses or the imagination. Bread and wine, — the commonest and plainest materials, — symbolical, as broken and poured, of great suffering, and also of sustenance and life through suffering, — a feast of most unpretending character; this is all, — this is the memorial of the love and anguish of our dear Lord. Divine and powerful in its simplicity. When faith is in exercise, what more do we need? Would not more be a hinderance rather than a help to our adoration?

Those simple elements are most congruous with a spiritual religion, which ever seeks to lift man up from the vulgar life of sense and sight, above the visible and the temporal; and also to give a right direction to his upward movement, so that he may not soar into the realm of mystical devovotion, but, on the wings of an intelligent and simple and spiritual faith, to holy and loving communion with Him who is all goodness, beauty, and truth; and may be incited to an humble, earnest, and faithful life of godliness. The religion of Christ is plain and simple, rebuking the pride and show of life, and especially pomp and fashion in religious worship, encouraging the practise of the simple virtues and lowly graces, and impressing upon us that its greatness and grandeur and glory are of the soul, in things invisible to mortal sight, in a likeness to Him whom no eye hath seen nor can see, whose name is Love.

It is evident, therefore, that for the right observance of this ordinance, as a feast of love, grateful and refreshing, there must be the preparation of a *spiritual mind*. Its power is in its symbolic character, and only a "spiritual discernment" can discover its meaning and bring out its hidden glory. Faith is indispensable, which can look through and beyond the simple outward signs to the great spiritual truths which are symbolized. Faith can discern the Lord's body and the great atonement. Faith can behold the living Christ, the adorable Lamb of God, and hold high communion with him.

But to find Christ there, we must carry him with us. A worldly mind will take the world to the Table, and retire as empty as it came.

There must be devout meditation and prayer, communion with Christ in the closet, in the Scriptures, in Christian duty, if we would derive comfort and strength from partaking of the Supper. To those who habitually walk with Christ, will he reveal himself with peculiar preciousness in the "breaking of bread."

Here is my heart,—my God, I give it thee;
　　I heard thee call and say,
"Not to the world, my child, but unto me;"—
　　I heard and will obey.
Here is love's offering to my King,
Which in glad sacrifice I bring,—
　　　　　Here is my heart!

Here is my heart;—surely the gift, though poor,
　　My God will not despise;
Vainly and long I sought to make it pure,
　　To meet thy searching eyes;
Corrupted once in Adam's fall,
The stains of sin pollute it all,—
　　　　　My guilty heart!

Here is my heart;—my heart so hard before,
　　Now by thy grace made meet;
Yet bruised and wearied, it can only pour
　　Its anguish at thy feet;
It groans beneath the weight of sin,
It sighs salvation's joy to win,—
　　　　　My mourning heart!

Here is my heart,—in Christ its longings end,
　　Near to the cross it draws;
It says, "Thou art my portion, O my Friend!
　　Thy blood my ransom was."
And in the Saviour it has found
What blessedness and peace abound,—
　　　　　My trusting heart!

THE MEMORIAL HOUR.

Here is my heart, — ah! Holy Spirit, come,
   Its nature to renew,
And consecrate it wholly as thy home,
   A temple fair and true.
Teach it to love and serve thee more,
   To fear thee, trust thee, and adore, —
         My cleansed heart!

Here is my heart; — it trembles to draw near
   The glory of thy throne;
Give it the shining robe thy servants wear,
   Of righteousness thine own;
Its pride and folly chase away,
   And all its vanity, I pray, —
         My humbled heart!

Here is my heart, — teach it, O Lord, to cling
   In gladness unto thee;
And in the day of sorrow still to sing,
   "Welcome, my God's decree;"
Believing, all its journey through,
   That thou art wise, and just and true, —
         My waiting heart!

Here is my heart, — O Friend of friends, be near
   To make the tempter fly;
And when my latest foe I wait with fear,
   Give me the victory!
Gladly on thy love reposing,
Let me say, when life is closing,
         "Here is my heart!"

True bread of life, in pitying mercy given,
　Long-famished souls to strengthen and to feed;
Christ Jesus, Son of God, true bread of heaven,
　Thy flesh is meat, thy blood is drink indeed.

I cannot famish, though this earth should fail;
　Though life, through all its fields, should pine and die;
Though the sweet verdure should forsake each vale,
　And every stream of every land run dry.

True Tree of life! of thee I eat and live;
　Who eateth of thy fruit shall never die;
'Tis thine the everlasting health to give,
　The youth and bloom of immortality.

Feeding on thee, all weakness turns to power,
　The sickly soul revives, like earth in spring;
Strength floweth on, and in each buoyant hour,
　This being seems all energy, all wing.

Jesus, our dying, buried, risen Head,
　Thy church's Life and Lord, Immanuel!
At thy dear cross we find the eternal bread,
　And in thy empty tomb the living well.

BONAR.

CHAPTER V.

THE MANNER OF OBSERVANCE—SUPERSTITIOUS VIEWS—POETRY.

"*Whatsoever is not of faith is sin.*"—*Rom.* 14:23.

A MOST solemn and profitable ordinance is the Lord's Supper in its "worthy" observance. But, like the doctrine of the cross, which it symbolizes, it is susceptible of perversion and desecration by the unspiritual communicant. And some, alas! we have reason to fear, come to the Table with a feeling of superstitious reverence, as if the material elements, by the words of consecration, were invested with a mysterious supernatural sacredness, and had virtue in themselves to work some magical influence on those who partake.

This is in part the error of the Romish church, which regards the bread and wine as actually changed by priestly consecration into the veritable body and blood of Christ, so that the communicant literally partakes of Christ, becomes physically incorporated into him, receiving, in the bread, his entire soul and body and divinity,— a most unscriptural perversion of the simple feast of love, and a gross misstatement of the believer's union with his Lord, and of the evangelical doctrine of regeneration and pardon and life.

In our Protestant communion it is to be feared, there are not a few who, if not accepting the precise Catholic dogma, yet do come to the Table with the feeling that to partake of the elements is an act of absolution, having virtue in itself to atone for sin, and affording indulgence to mingle again in the follies and fashions of the world,— an act of clearance for past offences and of license for future gratification. With solemn face,— not by necessity as hypocrites, but laboring under a sad delusion,— they come up from their worldly practices to the Lord's Table, put the bread and wine to their lips, and forthwith are relieved of a burden, and are light of heart; betrayed by their deceitful minds into the belief that they have performed a meritorious act and received a reward, while yet altogether blinded to their spiritual state and to the true method of justification; still in their sins and guilt, and, if possible, in a more hopeless condition.

The Lord's Supper was designed to be a memorial of *Christ*,— to lead our hearts to *him* in trust and love, as the sinner's only hope; but these deluded ones discern only the outward type, and confide in its inherent efficacy, or in their own act of participation as meritorious; drawn not toward Christ, but away from him; substituting the material for the spiritual, the sign for the thing signified. This is far more than an unfortunate mistake, it is a grievous and fatal error, a virtual rejection of Christ's atoning blood, an eating and drinking condemnation.

It overlooks the fact that unless Christ is received by the heart, in faith, he is not received at all; that no outward contact with anything that represents him, or that commemorates the most sacred mystery of his death, can for a moment effect any favorable change in our spiritual character or our standing with God; that such external communion with signs and types and memorials may be idolatry, and the more offensive to God because performed in the name of the Holy One, and with a professed acknowledgment of Christ as our redemption. "One name there is, and one alone, one alone in heaven and earth,— not truth, not justice, not benevolence, not Christ's mother, not his holiest servants, not his blessed sacraments, nor his very mystical body, the church; but himself only, who died for us and rose again, Jesus Christ, both God and man."[1]

The wooden cross on which our Saviour hung in agony was not thereby exalted above all the trees of the wood, and no portion of it has been allowed to remain as a snare to weak or worldly consciences. Were it in existence,— the identical cross,— placed erect within the reach and sight of men, there are multitudes who would "wonder after it," and from whose carnal eyes it would shut out the view of him who hung upon it, and whose sacrifice is the only cross we should seek and trust in.

Such is the fatal tendency to superstition, against which we need ever to be on our guard. By such mistaken views of the cross and the Supper, while seeming to have Calvary in our eye, we are hovering about Sinai, and are in peril of being consumed by its devouring flames. Professing to exalt Christ, we degrade him into a magi-

[1] Dr. Arnold. *Sermons.*

cian,— the bread is a stone and the wine poison. We drink the cup, not of salvation, but of death. The words of prayer and blessing over the elements are but empty incantations, to charm away from us the evil one. Christ has vanished from the feast. Satan looks with delight upon the vain mummeries which are binding stronger cords of death around his victims.

But danger also lies far inside these extreme mistakes and delusions. There is a universal tendency to exaggerate the value of external forms to satisfy conscience by some outward act in the place of faith, to substitute obedience for the merits and righteousness of Christ. Formality and self-righteousness are the greatest hindrances to devotion. Outward forms and symbols are needful, and even indispensable, and obedience is the test of faith; but the worship of the heart — the worship which recognizes and rests in Christ — is alone acceptable to God. "*Christ*," says Cecil, " is God's great ordinance."

Rightly viewed, the Lord's Supper is "spirit and life." It is not an empty form, leaving us as it found us. It helps to bring us into closer fellowship with the slain and risen Redeemer, to more and more endear him to our hearts, to invest sin with new loathsomeness, and holiness with fresh beauty. We cannot go forth from the Table, after thus remembering and receiving Christ, to be devotees of the world and slaves of sin. We feel that Heaven has come down to us in its infinite benignity to rebuke our sins, to pronounce our pardon, and to cheer us onward in the path of obedience and of life.

PRESERVE, my Jesus, oh preserve
  My soul to everlasting life.
Oh, may this blest communion serve
  To aid my soul in passion's strife.
Oh, may thy body, may thy blood,
Be to my soul a saving food,
To fill it still with life and grace,
And every sinful stain efface.

To bless thee be my sole employ,
  My God, my Saviour, great and kind!
Inflame my heart with holy joy;
  Teach me, in praising thee, to find
Warm thoughts and feelings warm, whose glow
My gratitude may aptly show.
But no, my God! nor word nor thought
Could bless and praise thee as I ought.

Weak praise were mine. Do thou inspire
My soul with love and living fire.
Oh may this cold and lowly breast
Be warmed by thee, its God, its guest!
May it by thee be moved to love,
And taught thy saving grace t' improve;
Take, then, my thoughts from all but thee:
  To thee may every impulse tend.

Dear Lord, may this communion prove
A never-failing bond of love.
Forgive my coldness, and supply
Mine every weak deficiency.
May the best grace suffice for all,
And every wayward sense enthrall;
Such grace on every feeling pour
As ne'er may leave thy servant more;
Each hope, each impulse firmly bind
In grace to thee, my Saviour kind;
Such saving grace, dear Lord, be given,
As leads the happy soul to heaven.
                        BESTE.

  OH, strong to save and bless,
  My Rock and Righteousness,
     Draw near to me!
  Blessing and joy and might,
  Wisdom and love and light,
     Are all with thee!

My Refuge and my Rest,
As child on mother's breast,
   I lean on thee.
From faintness and from fear,
When foes and ill are near,
   Deliver me!

Turn not away thy face,
Withhold not needed grace;
   My Fortress be!
Perils are round and round,
Iniquities abound;
   See, Saviour, see!

Come, God and Saviour, come!
I can no more be dumb;
   Appeal I must
To thee the gracious One,
Else is my hope all gone,
   I sink in dust!

Oh, answer me, my God!
Thy love is deep and broad,
   Thy grace is true!
Thousands this grace have shared,
Oh, let *me* now be heard,
   Oh, love *me* too.

Descend, thou mighty Love,
Descend from heaven above,
 Fill thou this soul!
Heal every bruised part,
Bind up this broken heart,
 And make me whole.

'Tis knowing thee that heals;
'Tis seeing thee that seals
 Comfort and peace.
Show me thy cross and blood,
My Saviour and my God,
 Then troubles cease.

BONAR.

CHAPTER VI.

ITS OBSERVANCE — FEELINGS OF DIFFERENT CLASSES OF CHRISTIANS — THE RIGHT SPIRIT — THANKSGIVING — POETRY.

"*He brought me to the banqueting-house, and his banner over me was love.*" — *Song of Solomon* 2 : 4.

IT is related in Jewish story that as a certain Rabbi and his companions were walking past the site of the Temple, they saw a fox come from amid its ruins, out of the Holy of Holies. At this sight *they* wept, but the Rabbi laughed and rejoiced. They wept, that in the place where, so holy was it, the stranger that drew near should die, now foxes walked upon it; he rejoiced, because as *this* prophecy was fulfilled, so would others be, which predicted brighter days to Zion. The ruin was prophetic of the rebuilding.

Here was the same scene, but how different the emotions which it awakened!

A company of Christians come to the Lord's Table, but their feelings are not all alike. It is the same Table for all, but not the same; for each one sheds over it the light or the shade of his own heart. Some regard it as a festival of love; their hearts overflow with gratitude and praise. Others are oppressed with a feeling of awful solemnity, as if a smile of gladness lighting up the face would be as unseemly as laughter at a funeral.

Is not the greater Temple — the very Holy of Holies — here represented as desecrated and destroyed by malicious hands? Is not this a death-scene, the most awful ever witnessed? Do we not gaze upon a broken body and streaming blood, all declaring the dreadful anguish of the sinless One, and ourselves his murderers?

How then can we do otherwise than bow with awful wonder and astonishment and shame, smiting our breasts in token of the bitterest self-accusation? Let others, if they can, rejoice; but we, wretched sinners, can only weep in sight of the cross on which we helped to nail the Prince of life. Is not human depravity here exhibited in its most repulsive aspect, in the commission of a crime unparalleled in all the dark annals of the world? Did not the sun refuse to look upon such a spectacle?

> "Oh, 'twas I — 'twas I that slew!
> I transpierced him, mocked him, spurned;
> I such love with hate returned!
> Spirit, that canst bid them flow,
> Touch the springs of holy woe!
> Let mine eyes as fountains be,
> Pouring tears incessantly,
> Like a deluge, down my cheek!
> Break this flinty heart, oh, break!"

How true, how far below the truth! and well may sinful man shudder at the thought of having participated in the guilt of crucifying the Lord of glory, or of being stained with sin which no blood less precious than that of Christ could wash away.

This is looking only at the ruins of the temple; this is forgetting that, in the Supper, we recognize the *raising* of the temple of Christ's body, and, in connection with that, the resurrection of dead souls from the ruins of the fall, and also the future resurrection of believers in the complete likeness of the great Restorer.

Christ is risen. Christ reigns. The veil of the temple was rent when Jesus died, and the sanctuary, even the Holy of Holies, — once open only for the high priest's consecrated feet on appointed days,—is now and ever accessible to all believers, through the blood shed upon the cross. That death of Christ was awful, but glorious; and our feelings of guilt and sadness should be transformed to gladness for that redemption which brings peace to man and new glory to God. The death of Christ is an event to rejoice in, to thank God for, in praises evermore. There is a fountain filled with blood, the most precious blood; but it has virtue to cleanse from the foulest stain of sin. It is a fountain of eternal life. With joy let us draw water from the wells of salvation. It is living water, springing up into everlasting life. Then far from the Lord's Table be the spirit of bondage. Christ died to set the captives free. Love should cast out fear. Let us rejoice in the God of our salvation. Let us lift up our heads and rejoice, knowing that our redemption draweth nigh. Now that Christ is risen, to live forever in the exercise of his eternal Priesthood, and in the full possession of that joy that was set before him, what glory do we see investing the cross! The shame is changed to glory. What transcendent love, what sweet grace, breathed out in those dying groans! What a glorious victory achieved over sin and all the infernal powers! What new joy through all the realms of the blest!

The early Christians gloried in the death of Christ. It was the theme not only of preaching but of song. Everything great, noble, tender, god-like, centred in the cross. "God forbid," exclaimed an apostle, "that I should glory, save in the cross of our Lord Jesus Christ." By it man is saved, Satan confounded, and God glorified. The thought of that cross of shame and agony expelled from their hearts the fear of man, and fired them with a noble courage in efforts to spread the story of redemption.

Hence they were wont to celebrate the death of Christ, in the Supper, as an occasion not of sadness but of joy. They came together to the feast of love to renew their strength in a remembrance of Him who, of all, loved them most, who had died for them, and who, now risen, was interceding for them and watching over them, — their best Friend, their elder Brother, their Saviour, and their Lord.

It is true, we should, with every remembrance of Christ, think of our sin with shame and contrition; but no longer as under condemnation.

Faith in the Christ who died passes us over from

death to life. We are complete in Christ. We are safe in Christ. We are heirs of God and joint-heirs with Christ.

Constitutional differences show themselves in the realm of religion. The mind projects its own lights and shadows over the field of contemplation, and thus one walks in the sunshine, another under a cloud, the same heavens the while bending over them.

Sometimes a conscience morbidly sensitive perpetually suggests reasons for self-accusation, so that Hope suffers an eclipse, and Fear draws a cloud over the scene which of all others should shine with a heavenly radiance.

If the mind takes a partial and narrow view, looking almost exclusively at the present scene, at the physical suffering and the human guilt, as the friends of the Rabbi thought only of the desolation that met the eye, and not also of the future' glory which that ruin prophesied, then the Lord's Supper awakens only feelings of sadness or dread. But that scene utters ever a sweet prophecy of a glory that shall be revealed.

Weakness of faith is perhaps the most frequent cause of religious despondency, and of the sadness with which the Lord's Table is sometimes approached. This feebleness of faith circumscribes the vision, and occasions limited and insufficient views of the atonement, and of the relation of sin to the Kingdom of grace. But faith, when in lively exercise, sees in that which, but for Christ, would awaken ceaseless and bitter tears, the occasion of a higher joy. Earth and heaven,—even the abyss of hell; time and eternity; sin and holiness; guilt and redemption; man's malice and God's overruling providence and overmastering, superabounding grace, pass before Faith's wide and deep-seeing eye, and the soul rises to that serener height where all conflicting elements are hushed to peace,—that sacred calm which is the foretaste of eternal rest. To the eye of faith thus instructed, the Lord's Supper is not a funeral scene, suggestive only of death and woe. If Christ sang on his way to the cross, surely we may sing, now that he has passed from the cross to the throne, "leading captivity captive, and giving gifts to men."[1]

"The death of Christ is the most amazing event that ever took place in the universe, and therefore the Lord's Supper is the most amazing of all ordinances. The angels desire to look into it. I

[1] Eph. iv. 8.

doubt not that the angels hover round the communion table, and sing their sweetest praises to the Lord when they see the bread broken and the wine poured out."[1]

"There is nothing to surround the Lord's Table with gloom. We are not called unto the mount covered with clouds and darkness, from which issue the signs of wrath, but unto Mount Zion, to the abode of mercy and grace, where all is love, — the dying love of Him who never breaks the bruised reed."[2]

"Let the disconsolate, lamenting sinner," says the saintly, sainted Leighton, "lift up his head and behold Christ, the Son of God, anointed a *prophet*, to preach to such salvation and liberty, a *priest*, to purchase it, and a *king*, to give it."

We dishonor God, we detract from the sweet glories of the cross, we introduce discord into the hymns of Paradise, we are chargeable with ingratitude, when we celebrate God's unspeakable gift with feelings of solemn gloom.

[1] McCheyne. *Sermons.*   [2] Dr. Hodge. *Com. on Cor.*

Oh, show me not my Saviour dying,
　As on the cross he bled;
Nor in the tomb a captive lying,
　For he has left the dead.
Then bid me not that form extended
　For my Redeemer own,
Who to the highest heavens ascended,
　In glory fills the throne.

Weep not for him at Calvary's station,
　Weep only for thy sins;
View where he lay with exultation;
　'Tis there our hope begins.
Yet stay not there, thy sorrows feeding,
　Amid the scenes he trod;
Look up and see him interceding
　At the right hand of God.

Still in the shameful cross I glory,
　Where his dear blood was spilt;
My soul is melted at the story
　Of him who bore my guilt.
Yet what, 'mid conflict and temptation,
　Shall strength and succor give?
He lives, the Captain of salvation!
　Therefore his servants live.

By death, he death's dark king defeated,
　And overcame the grave;
Rising, the triumph he completed:
　He lives, he reigns to save!

Heaven's happy myriads bow before him;
  He comes, the Judge of men:
These eyes shall see him and adore him;
  Lord Jesus! own me then.
CONDER.

In thy cross is all my plea;
By thy bonds am I made free;
By thy stripes my soul is healed;
By thy blood my pardon sealed.

By thy fainting I endure;
By thy fall I stand secure;
By thy cruel death I live; —
Joy and peace thy sufferings give.

By thy fasting I am fed
Richly with a living bread!
By thy thirsting, through my soul,
Living waters ever roll.

By that cruel crown of thorns,
Holy peace my brow adorns;
By those mocking taunts and jeers,
I am saved from shame and tears.

Just, by Jesus justified,
When beneath my sins he died!
Righteous, by thy righteousness,
Thine own robe my perfect dress!

Perfect, by thy perfect life;
Peaceful, by thy holy strife;
Pure, by Jesus purified,
In the fountain from thy side.

Holy, by thy holiness,
Resting by thy weariness;
By thy sorrow I may sing,
From thy groans my pleasure spring!

Thou wast poor; how rich am I!
Thou wast homeless,— Jesus, why?
Only that my soul might share
Mansions here and mansions there!

By thy rising, I shall rise;
Death must yield its transient prize;
Thine ascension mine shall be;
All thy glory I shall see!

Cross of Christ! here, *here* I fall,
Pleading only, CHRIST IS ALL;
This, my God, my Judge, shall be
At thy bar *my only plea!*

      H. HAMLIN.

CHAPTER VII.

ITS OBSERVANCE — THE DOUBTING AND FEARFUL — ENCOURAGE-
MENT — EATING AND DRINKING UNWORTHILY — POETRY.

"A bruised reed shall he not break, and the smoking flax shall he not quench." — *Isaiah* 52 : 3.

OUR gracious Lord has set his Table in the wilderness, in order to cheer and invigorate his redeemed in the house of their pilgrimage. Thither he invites the weary and heavy-laden. He himself is present, the Master of the feast and the Feast itself; the compassionate Friend, the Bread of life.

And yet there are not a few of Christ's professed disciples whom a deep sense of unworthiness brings to the Table with a painful hesitancy, perhaps causes them even to sit apart and look mournfully on, while others, better, they think, than themselves, are partaking of the emblems of the Redeemer's love. Oh, how precious and glorious in their sight is this emblematic feast, and how they wish that they had a right to be among the favored guests! but their sins and imperfections are like a flaming sword, forbidding them a place within the sacred enclosure. Their tender consciences, brooding over the past, so dark to their view with duties neglected and privileges abused, and over their hearts, so hard and insensible to their Saviour's love, build a wall around the Table spread by his hands, so that they dare only to look over with conflicting emotions, or else seem to themselves to force an entrance because they dare not stay without.

How often, when the invitation to the Supper is extended, would many a professing Christian, rather than remain and take to his lips the bread and wine, withdraw with the worldly crowd, though his heart really lingers behind, and go home to weep over his sins, were it not that his conduct would attract observation, or be attributed to some cause that would be painful to his feelings as perhaps dishonoring to Christ. Could he steal out, silent and unnoticed, gladly would he do it. And then he charges himself with hypocrisy for remaining from such a motive, and seems to himself to be drinking condemnation. He thinks he will never do the like again: that he will, before the next communion season, ask to be set aside from the church as an unworthy member, and thus have the temptation removed to profane the holy Supper.

But something in his heart forbids such a step. The church is still his chosen habitation, where alone he can be happy; and again he is drawn to the Lord's Table.

But he lives in fear. He is not the rejoicing disciple that he should be.

Let me speak to you, dear doubting one, with the plainness and affection of a friend, with Christian fidelity and kindness.

You fear to sit at the Lord's Table because of your unworthiness. You feel that you are very sinful, and that it would be adding to your guilt to place yourself there. But would you be numbered with the world? Would you choose their society and their pleasures? Your heart, after all, is with the people of God, with those who love and honor Christ? Will you, then, do violence to these deepest convictions of your heart, which have drawn, and still draw you, to the church of Christ, as your really chosen home? Will you turn from the disciples of Christ, especially when they would testify their peculiar love to him who, as head of the church and its indwelling life, gives to the church its attractive power?

You are unworthy. This is your plea. Tell me, then, to whom, when sin presses hard upon your conscience, and forces from you the cry, "Oh, wretched man that I am, who shall deliver me from the body of this death?" do you go for help? Do you not exclaim, "I thank God, *through Jesus Christ our Lord?*" Does not your heart go out after Jesus, as your only refuge? after his precious blood, to cleanse you from sin? Do you not feel that by longer waiting, or by personal performances, you can never prepare yourself for a worthier approach? that if you go at all, you must go as you are, crying,—

>Just as I am, without one plea
>But that thy blood was shed for me,
>And that thou bid'st me come to thee,
>   O Lamb of God, I come!

>Just as I am, and waiting not
>To rid my soul of one dark blot,
>To thee whose blood can cleanse each spot,
>   O Lamb of God, I come!

Say, do you not feel that you must go all needy, all helpless, to *receive everything* from Jesus?

Well, O professed disciple, what shall forbid your going to the Lord's Table? You will find him there, and in the most winning, welcoming attitude. *Remember me* is the language of the ordinance, or rather of Christ in the ordinance. Behold the memorials of my blood shed for sin,— for *your* sin,— for the very sins which have made you fear to approach. Do not the broken bread and the poured-out wine say to you, " Come unto me, and I will give you rest"?

If Christ, in his person, bleeding from the fresh wounds of his crucifixion, were passing by, would or should the deepest sense of guilt and unworthiness prevent you from going to him for pardon? Would you not hasten to him, and, falling at his blessed, bleeding feet, and looking up into that face bearing still the traces of anguish yet radiant with love and pity, press your suit with all the earnestness of one who knew that he could not be denied?

Does not the Lord's Supper " show the death" of Christ, show him in his blood, waiting to be gracious, stretching out his arms to receive you?

ENCOURAGEMENT. 87

'Is not this ordinance designed to be a help to faith, that you may look and live?

Oh, if there is one place of all which would seem to win to itself the trembling Christian, weighed down under a sense of unworthiness, it is the memorial feast; for it is a feast of love,—of love unutterable and unto death. It is love that spreads the Table, love that invites you to it; and if you turn away with the thought that for such sinners as you it cannot have been provided, what do you,—oh, think of it!—but question the immensity and sincerity of that love and the all-sufficiency of that great sacrifice? " There is an offer of friendship on His part, let it be accepted on ours; and the acceptance lies in our firm reliance on the honesty of the offer. Let us not stagger at a privilege so infinitely above our merits and our hopes being brought so wonderfully nigh unto us; but against hope, against all the likelihoods of nature and experience, let us believe in hope. Such faith, even though we thereby arrogate to our own sinful selves the greatest and highest of all blessings, has no arrogance and no presumption at all in it. It has another character altogether. It is yielding due honor to one of the divine attributes, even the attribute of Truth; so that the stronger the faith, the greater is the glory we render unto God. What a precious harmony is this, that our greatest peace and God's greatest glory are at one,— that in counting him faithful who has promised, we do that which at one and the same time most advances his honor and most tranquillizes our own fears. Rebuke, then, away from us, O God, all the doubtings of unbelief as well as its distinctions."[1]

You still speak of your unworthiness. But was the Lord's Table spread for angels,— the pure, the sinless, the elder-born who never strayed from their Father's house? Not for them this feast. They are not called to it. They can only look on and wonder. It is for sinners, the chief of sinners, the deserving heirs of wrath. The banished ones are invited.

And are you not a sinner? This is your greatest argument. But how futile here, since you confess your sin.

To partake, then, as a sinner, is not to be a hypocrite, for you come not as self-righteous, but as self-condemned.

You need Christ. Behold him here. Out from his baptism of anguish, with garments dyed in

---

[1] Dr. Chalmers. *Daily Scripture Readings.*

blood, with pierced hands outspread to bid the conscious, confessing sinner welcome, he speaks to you in this ordinance.

"Almighty God stands by the body of his lifeless son, and says, as well he may, 'What could I have done more for you than I have done?' More he could not do, though there had been as many crosses as hills on earth, and a cross on every hill, and an angel nailed on every cross. Yon single cross, yon middle tree of Calvary, was greater than them all! More he could not do! And what can *you* say? Father, my Father which art in heaven, I have sinned against thee! Give me thy precious Son! give me thy gracious Spirit! give me Jesus, else I die!'"[1]

A Nestorian Christian lady, wishing to commune with the American missionaries, appeared before them for examination concerning her knowledge of Christ. Her heart was overflowing with love and joy. To test her profession, a missionary asked her:—"Would you still trust in the grace of God if your present joy were taken from you and you were left in darkness?"

"Certainly I would," she replied.

"And what would you do if we were to refuse

[1] Dr. Guthrie.

you admission to the Table of our Lord?" asked the missionary.

"I should rejoice the more in the Lord Jesus," said the lady.

"Why so?"

"Why, if all my friends cast me off, and you, too, *to whom could I go but to him?* I would cling more to him than ever!"

"*I would cling more to him than ever!*"

Cling to Christ, then, O troubled Christian.

But my faith is so weak. "Faith," however, as a pious man has said, "is not always a burning torch,— it is often only a glimmering taper. The taper gives light as well as the torch, but the light is not so strong. Faith is the eye with which we see Jesus. A small eye is still an eye, and a weeping eye is still an eye."[1]

"There is a story how the Devil appeared to a dying man, and showed him a parchment roll, which was very long, wherein was written on every side the sins of the poor sick man, which were many in number; and there were also written the idle words he had spoken in his life, together with the false words, the unchaste words, and angry words; afterwards came his vain and

---

[1] Tholuck. *Hours of Devotion.*

ungodly words; and, lastly, his actions digested according to the commandments. Whereupon Satan said, 'See here, behold thy virtues; see here what thy examination must be.' Whereupon the poor sinner answered, 'It is true; but thou hast not set down all, for thou shouldst have added, and set down here below, THE BLOOD OF JESUS CHRIST CLEANSETH FROM ALL SIN. And this also should not have been forgotten,—WHOSOEVER BELIEVETH IN HIM SHALL NOT PERISH, BUT HAVE EVERLASTING LIFE;' whereupon the Devil vanished. Thus, if the Devil should muster up our sins, and set them in order before us, let but Christ be named in a faithful way, and he will give back and fly away with all speed.

> 'My sins are great, I do confess,
> And of a scarlet dye;
> But Jesus' blood can wash me clean,
> As God does testify.'" [1]

My reason, you answer, tells me this is true. I believe that the blood of Jesus Christ cleanseth from all sin; but when the hour arrives for celebrating the Supper, that fearful passage in the First Epistle to the Corinthians, about eating and

[1] *Golden Treasury.*

drinking unworthily, and being guilty of the body and blood of the Lord, and eating and drinking damnation, makes me tremble lest I should fall under that terrible condemnation. You do well, dear believer, to examine yourself ere you come to the Lord's Table. But the class here referred to are such as "come in a careless and irreverent spirit, without the intention or desire to commemorate the death of Christ as the sacrifice for sin, and without the purpose of complying with the engagements which are thereby assumed. The warning is against the careless and profane, and not against the timid and the doubting."[1] "To eat and drink with a consciousness of unworthiness, with a sense of ill-desert, is one of the conditions of acceptable communion." The Table is provided not for the strong and self-reliant, but for bruised reeds, for such as cannot stand in their own strength, but must lean somewhere, and know no other arm so strong and safe as the arm of the Beloved. Come, then, where that strong arm of love is made bare, and whence proceed the gracious words, — "Remember me." Those words are not only a command enjoining a duty, but they tenderly beseech you, in your weakness, hopeless

---

[1] Dr. Hodge. Com. 1 Cor.

of human succor, to lean the weight of your misery upon His loving bosom. "Remember ME."

Amid the shadows and the fears
That overcloud this home of tears,
Amid my poverty and sin,
The tempest and the war within,
    I cast my soul on thee,
    Mighty to save even me,
    Jesus, thou Son of God!

Drifting across a sunless sea,
Cold, heavy mists encurtaining me;
Toiling along life's broken road,
With snares around and foes abroad,
    I cast my soul on thee,
    Mighty to save even me,
    Jesus, thou Son of God!

Mine is a day of fear and strife,
A needy soul, a needy life,
A needy world, a needy age;
Yet, in my perilous pilgrimage,
    I cast my soul on thee,
    Mighty to save even me,
    Jesus, thou Son of God!

To thee I come, — ah, only thou
Canst wipe the sweat from off this brow;
Thou, only thou, canst make me whole,
And soothe the fever of my soul;
    I cast my soul on thee,
    Mighty to save even me,
    Jesus, thou Son of God!

On thee I rest; thy love and grace
Are my sole rock and resting-place;
In thee, my thirst and hunger sore,
Lord, let me quench for evermore.
    I cast my soul on thee,
    Mighty to save even me,
    Jesus, thou Son of God!

'Tis earth, not heaven! 'tis night, not noon;
The sorrowless is coming soon;
But till the morn of love appears,
Which ends the travail and the tears,
    I cast my soul on thee,
    Mighty to save even me,
    Jesus, thou Son of God!

Ah, Jesus, why should I complain?
  And why fear aught but sin?
Distractions are but outward things;
  Thy peace dwells far within!

POETRY.

These surface-troubles come and go,
  Like rufflings of the sea;
The deeper depth is out of reach
  To all, my God, but thee!
              FABER.

Down from the willow bough
  My slumbering harp I'll take,
And bid its silent strings
  To heavenly themes awake;—
Peaceful let its breathings be,
When I sing of Calvary.

Love, LOVE DIVINE, I sing;
  Oh for a seraph's lyre,
Bathed in Siloa's stream,
  And touched with living fire;
Lofty, pure, the strain should be
When I sing of Calvary.

Love, *Love* on earth appears!
  The wretched throng his way;
He beareth all their griefs,
  And wipes their tears away.
Soft and sweet the strain should be,
Saviour, when I sing of thee.

He saw me as he passed,
　In hopeless sorrow lie,
Condemned and doomed to death,
　And no salvation nigh;
Loud and long the strain should be
When I sing his love to me.

"I die for thee," he said;
　Behold the cross arise!
And lo! he bows his head,—
　He bows his head and dies!
Soft, my harp, thy breathings be;
Let me weep on Calvary.

He lives! again he lives!
　I hear the voice of love,
He comes to soothe my fears
　And draw my soul above;
Joyful now the strain should be
When I sing of Calvary.

MRS. SOUTHEY.

Thou precious head, with thorny crown,
　Since thou with us didst so unite
That all our grief became thine own;
　Ah, we can never tell aright,—
Nay, scarcely even can believe
The strength we now from thee receive.

CHAPTER VIII.

THE SUPPER A WITNESS AGAINST SIN — HUMILITY AND CONFESSION — POETRY.

"Reckon ye yourselves to be dead indeed unto sin, but alive unto God through Jesus Christ our Lord. — Rom. 6 : 11.

WHILE the Lord's Supper exhibits an infinite compassion for sinners, it also exhibits an infinite abhorrence of sin. This last aspect of the ordinance should never be obscured, lest the divine beneficence be "degraded into a reckless infinitude of mercy, a blind obliteration of sin;" and so at length mercy itself be eclipsed, and all the glory of the cross vanish away. For if sin be not an infinite evil, if it be more a calamity than a crime, a misfortune than a fault, calling rather for pity than punishment, — then where the tran-

[1] Ruskin. *Modern Painters.*

scendent grace of the gospel? Why did angels fly from their celestial homes to sing "good-will to men," over the plains of Bethlehem?

So far is the death of Christ, in its declaration of God's love, from weakening our sense of his justice, that it exhibits that justice as pouring out the vials of its wrath upon the head of the Substitute of guilty men. The Crucifixion is God's look of terrible indignation, the letting loose his awful thunderbolts, the unsheathing of the sword of justice and bathing it in blood. Sin is a tremendous fact, which no manifestation of pity on the part of God either can, or is designed to look out of sight, but which that pity, as breathed forth so sweetly on Calvary, stamps with the seal of a more terrible reprobation.

O Lamb of God! louder than Sinai's thunderings does thy meek and silent agony proclaim the exceeding sinfulness of sin.

With what profound humility and self-loathing should a believer partake of the memorials of that tremendous sacrifice, which at once declared the infinite guilt of his sin and relieved him of its crushing burden,— which reveals grace as reigning through righteousness unto eternal life, sparing not the only-begotten, but giving him up to tread the wine-press alone. The believer, "saved from wrath through him," should indeed regard the Supper as a festival of love, from which all thoughts of fear and gloom should be excluded; but his joy is that of deliverance not from a misfortune but from a deserved wrath; not from an abyss into which an inexorable and irresponsible fate, but his own evil passions, were drifting him. And his joy is tempered, while heightened even to rapture, by the fact that the curse from which he is saved fell upon the innocent and holy Lamb of God,— that by the overwhelming sorrows of his Substitute he is permitted to dwell in peace. Self-exaltation can never mingle with a believer's bliss. Even when he has reached the land of Beulah, with its cloudless skies and its sweet music through all the day and night, with its perfect peace and the companionship of the "shining ones;" even here, on the borders of heaven, will he remember the hole of the pit whence he was drawn, and this shall clothe him with humility, while he thinks of the wonderful condescension of grace. As he sits at the Lord's Table, he sees that the hand of infinite Pity which is reached forth to save him bears the marks of the divine wrath against his sin.

And may it not be that with the believer's joy in heaven shall be mingled a feeling akin to sadness, yet not such as involves unhappiness, being a sadness so pure, so unselfish, so connecting itself with Christ's infinite sympathy as to lend a strange sweetness to his joy, and even swell it to rapture?

"There is not any part of our feeling or nature, nor can there be through eternity, which shall not be in some way influenced and affected by the fall, and that not in any way of degradation, for the renewing in the divinity of Christ is a nobler condition than even that of Paradise; and yet, throughout eternity it must imply and refer to the disobedience, and the corrupt state of sin and death, and the suffering of Christ himself, which can we conceive of any redeemed soul as for an instant forgetting or as remembering without sorrow? Neither are the alternations of joy and such sorrow as by us is inconceivable, being only as it were a softness and silence in the pulse of an infinite felicity, inconsistent with the state even of the unfallen, for the angels who rejoice over repentance cannot but feel an uncomprehended pain as they try and try again in vain whether they may not warm hard hearts with the brooding of their kind wings."[1]

At the Lord's Table it becomes us to renew and deepen our abhorrence of sin, and to form new resolutions to strive against it in all its forms, as that abominable thing from which he came to save his people, through the suffering of death. How can we go from the cross to be on terms of friendship with the murderers of the Crucified? How can we cherish in our hearts that which broke the heart of Jesus? How can we indulge in pride and vanity, in sight of the memorials, as of the divine love, so of our own shame?

But while, in the light of the cross, we see the hatefulness of sin, so also on the dark ground of human depravity, the sweet grace of Christ reveals its rainbow hues in their infinite loveliness. While, therefore, we deplore our guilt and misery as past all human cure, we can rejoice the more in that *free* forgiveness which greets us in our hopeless ruin, in that full salvation which meets the utmost emergency of our case, the *gift* of God through Jesus Christ. The very sense of our sin and ruin as desperate and overwhelming, prepares us to appreciate the value of the provisions of the gospel,

---

[1] Ruskin, *Modern Painters*, Vol. II., p. 117.

and to experience a feeling of peace and repose and blissful confidence of which a sinner saved by grace alone can be conscious.

Flow, my tears, flow still faster,
   Thus my guilt and sin bemoan;
Mourn, my heart, in deeper anguish,
   Over sorrows not thine own!
See a spotless Lamb draw nigh
To Jerusalem to die;
For thy sins, the sinless One;
Think, ah! think what thou hast done!

See him stand while cruel fetters
   Bind the hands that framed the world,
While around him bitter mocking,
   Laughter and contempt are hurled.
Heathen rage and Jewish scorn
Meekly for our sins are borne.
Sin has brought him from above;
Who can fathom such a love?

Soon the heavy doom is spoken,
   Even Pilate's pleading ceased,
Jesus to the cross is chosen,
   And Barabbas is released!

Ah! there is no loving word,
Not one voice of pity heard!
But the loud and frenzied cry,—
"Crucify him!—crucify!"

Can we view the Saviour given
   To the smiter's hands for us?
Can we all unmoved, unhumbled,
   See him mocked and slighted thus?
View the thorny chaplet made
For his meek and silent head,
Hear the loud and angry din,
And not tremble for our sin?

Follow from the hall of judgment
   This sad Saviour on his way;
But in spirit, as ye journey,
   Often pause and humbly pray;—
Pray the Father to behold
By the Son thy ransom told,
And a Substitute for thee,
In his well-beloved see!

Must I, Jesus, thus behold thee
   In thy toil and sorrow here?
Can I nothing better yield thee
   Than my unavailing tear?

Lamb of God, I weep for thee!
Weep, thy cruel cross to see!
Weep, for death that death destroys!
Weep, for grief that brings me joys!

Poor is all that I can offer,—
  Soul and body while I live;
Take it, O my Saviour, take it,—
  I have nothing more to give.
Come, and in this heart remain;
Let each enemy be slain;
Let me live and die with thee;
To thy kingdom welcome me.

Loud and louder saints are singing,
  Glory! glory! Christ, to thee!
Over death and hell forever
  Thou hast triumphed gloriously.
I am thine, and thou art mine;
Oh, to see thy brightness shine!
Lord, thy day of grief is o'er,
Come in glory,—come once more!

LAURENTIUS LAURENTI. *Hymns from the Land of Luther.*

Lord! at thy table we behold
  The wonders of thy grace;
But most of all admire that we
  Should find a welcome place;—

We, who are all defiled with sin,
    And rebels to our God!
We, who have crucified thy Son,
    And trampled on his blood!

What strange, surprising grace is this,
    That we, so lost, have room;
Jesus our weary souls invites,
    And freely bids us come.

Ye saints below, and hosts above!
    Join all your sacred powers;
No theme is like redeeming love,
    No Saviour is like ours.
                  STENNETT.

THOU great Redeemer, who for us hast bled,
In trespasses and sins our hearts were dead;
But since thy pardoning grace new life can give,
Then, gracious Saviour, oh, my sins forgive!
Where'er a streamlet of thy grace is found,
There will the tender flowers and fruits abound;
And oh, how deeply in my soul I feel
That *grace alone* my wretched state can heal.

CHAPTER IX.

THE DEATH OF CHRIST A CENTRAL FACT — ITS RELATION TO THE SEVERAL OFFICES OF CHRIST — POETRY.

"Ye do show the Lord's Death till he come." — 1 Cor. 11 : 26.

AN eminent divine has said "What is the history of the world without Christ?"[1] He is its central figure, — "the sovereign intervention of divine love in history." With reference to him, all that preceded his coming was a prophecy and preparation, and all that followed, a revelation.

And the *death* of Christ is the central fact and vital element of his whole redemptive work. It is the key which unlocks the mystery of his incarnation. It interprets all the events of his life, gives value and glory to all his offices, and invests his

[1] Julius Müller.

second coming with surpassing interest. "Both historically and doctrinally, the Passion appears as the central and crowning point of the gospel."[1]

It is remarkable that the four Gospels are not so much a biography as an obituary,—a record of the closing portion of Christ's life. His birth and childhood are briefly noticed; the many years that follow—forming the larger part of his life on earth—are passed over almost in silence, until we come to the last three or four, upon which the pen of inspiration dwells with a minuteness and fulness that indicate the vast importance of those final years and their vital connection with his mission to mankind, the interest of the narrative deepening toward the end, nearly eight chapters of one evangelist, seven of another, and five each of two others, being devoted to an account of the last week. How the sacred writers linger about the last two days!—days crowded with events, all connected with and declaring the preëminent importance of the crucifixion of our Lord. His whole earthly life is, in itself, subordinate to his death.

His decease cannot therefore be regarded as merely the natural termination of a human life,

---

[1] Westcott. *Introd. to the Study of the Gospels.*

inevitable to our common humanity; nor, considered as a violent end of his work, was it the mere seal and testimony of his sincerity.

It was an event *for* which, preëminently, he became incarnate, the predestined end which he ever kept steadily in view through all his ministry as the consummation and crown of that ministry. *He came* TO DIE, to give up his life a ransom, to lay down his life for his sheep, to shed that blood without which there could be no remission of sins. His solemn utterance upon the cross, "*It is finished!*" "suggests the idea of a prescribed, a distinct, a definite work, brought to a final, satisfactory, and triumphant conclusion. . . . . . Taking it as the simple announcement of the fact that some great transaction was brought to its consummation, we ask ourselves, as we contemplate the entire circle of the Redeemer's services to our race, still running out their course, what part of these services was it of which it could be said that it was finished? Here, in the foreground, we have to put that one and perfect sacrifice which he offered up for the sin of the world. Through the Eternal Spirit he offered himself without spot to God, and by that one sacrifice for sin, once for all, he hath perfected forever those that are sanctified;

he hath done all that was needed to atone for human guilt, to redeem us from the curse of the law, to finish transgression, to make an end of sin, to make reconciliation for iniquity." [1]

To understand, then, the life and mission of Christ, we must take our stand at the cross, and from that, as from a high mount of observation, survey all that preceded and all that followed or is yet to come. Viewed from that point, everything falls into place, and every distinct feature contributes to the symmetry and completeness of the whole. A beauty and glory radiate from the cross to spread over the entire field of vision. Our sense of fitness is not violated but satisfied by the appearance of angelic hosts at the Saviour's birth; their songs of rapture seem not mythical interpolations to give dignity to the story of that birth, but natural and spontaneous utterances, revealing a sympathy which must be felt through all the realms of the blest and holy, in the redemption of the lost in whatever part of the universe, so that we are persuaded the mystery would rather lie in the absence and silence of these heavenly visitants.

Looking out from the cross, the *life* of Christ develops new beauty and significance. It is a life

[1] Dr. Hanna. *Last Day of our Lord's Passion.*

of obedience, whose every moment was a part of that great sacrifice finished on Calvary; which was preparing the way for that last great act, and giving it a virtue and glory which it could not otherwise have had.

What beauty and power does the *example* of Christ derive from his atoning death! It is the example of him through whose blood we have redemption. The irresistible inference of grace and gratitude is, "Walk in love, as Christ also hath loved us and given himself for us."

No less human is his life because he was also more than man; no less true and valuable his example because he was more than pattern, even a Redeemer. The steps which he traced in the world, as he went about doing good, all tended to the cross of expiation, *that* making those steps radiant with a strange glory which wins the believer to walk in them. A holy life is an imitation of Christ; the imitation of Christ springs from love to Christ; and love to Christ from his great love to us in dying for our redemption. Thus intimate is the connection between the death of Christ and holy living, between the office of Christ as Redeemer and his office as Example.

Christ reveals himself as our *Friend and Brother.*

And a true brother is he in the purity, tenderness, faithfulness, constancy, and far-reaching influence of his friendship.

But what is it that casts over all his brotherly life a light so sadly beautiful, so strangely winning? *It is the Cross.* There did our brother *die*, proving by that act the immeasurable depths of his love, in the agony and shame he was so ready to endure for our welfare. His love staggered at no sacrifice.

And when we consider that his was a death of propitiation, to atone for and remove man's greatest misery and the source of all his woes — sin, — we see how unspeakably valuable is his friendship, which reaches beyond the confines of time into eternity. What can he not, what will he not, do for the happiness of those who seek his friendship?

Christ is a *Teacher*. He is the *great* Teacher, speaking as never man spake, both as to the matter and the spirit of his instructions. Not a stern, severe teacher, exacting hard lessons to be learned by our painful, solitary toil, and roughly rebuking our imperfections and failures, our dull perceptions and slow progress. He is meek and lowly in heart, he condescends to our weakness, he bears with our numerous mistakes, he tenderly reproves our dulness, he sweetly encourages us forward, he patiently repeats the lessons we had failed to learn, he perfectly understands our difficulties, and adapts himself to our peculiarities of character and condition.

But how is it that Christ is so incomparable a teacher? It is not enough to say that he is divine,—that he knows all things. The Cross alone explains it. Our *Saviour* is our Teacher. As he draws us to sit with him beneath the tree of agony, we wonder not that he who condescended to so great a shame and sorrow for our salvation, should also, with meekness and patience, lead us on to the attainment of that divine knowledge which is necessary to the complete realization of the benefits included in that salvation. To know Christ himself is also the greatest wisdom, to become more and more perfectly acquainted with him in whom are hid all the treasures of wisdom and knowledge; and where can we study Christ as at the cross? His death is a wondrous revelation, declaring the "manifold wisdom of God." When Jesus draws us to his side, and shows us the marks of the nails and the spear, we learn what no wisdom of earth could teach us, *of God and of our-*

selves. Here we learn *what sin is*, and *what is its perfect cure*.

At the cross, Jesus teaches the great lessons of *duty to God and man*, and writes upon the heart the motives which constitute obedience and make that obedience freedom. How wondrously he there unfolds the character of God, especially in its holiness and love, to win us to his worship and service; and how tenderly he teaches at once the sinfulness and dignity of man, irrespective of race or condition, to inculcate brotherly love. Who *can* teach the lessons of religion and humanity as Christ can?

At the cross, Christ *interprets and justifies the Providence of God*, inasmuch as there we learn, in that example of infinite mercy which spared not the well-beloved Son but delivered him up for us all, that, notwithstanding all the dark mysteries of Providence, Righteousness and Love do reign supreme and that all things must work together for good to them that love God. Jesus alone teaches us to say, in the deepest gloom, when in the entire field of human vision there is discernible not one glimmer of hope, All is well, — God reigns, — justice will triumph, *for Christ has died*. Calvary stands, and shall forever stand, to refute all accusations against the goodness and justice of God, and to calm the fears of his sorrowing children.

Christ is *Mediator*, through whom alone guilty man can have access to his injured and offended Sovereign. But what is the ground of his mediation? what constitutes it an effectual step to a satisfactory and complete reconciliation? The answer comes in connection with the inspired announcement of this office of Christ: "There is one mediator between God and man,—the man Christ Jesus, who *gave himself a ransom* for all." His death, as the price of redemption, was the ground of mediation. God, as Creator and King, can accept this sacrifice without any compromise of his honor or authority, and man can, therefore, be at liberty to approach his Maker, with the promise of acceptance and pardon.

Christ is *Advocate;* at the right hand of God he makes intercession for us : and this is also a part of his mediatorial work. He there pleads the cause of his ransomed people as one personally interested in their welfare, answering all charges entered against them, and insuring their triumphant vindication and final salvation.

But why is he an Advocate whom "the Father

heareth always"? why do his intercessions make so irresistible an appeal? what are the considerations which he presents in behalf of his people, that they should so outweigh all the objections which, from whatever quarter, might be brought against them?

The Cross answers these questions. Christ *pleads the merits of his death.* That precious blood which he shed for the life of his people, he holds up before the throne of Eternal Justice, and this prevails. "It is Christ that died." What more can be demanded? The sheep for whom he *laid down his life* shall still have a Shepherd's care through all their way in the wilderness, until they enter the heavenly fold. They were given to Christ in eternal covenant, the bond was sealed in blood, and who shall break the seal? Therefore shall their great Surety, as their Advocate, gain for them pardon and peace, and the continual supply of grace unto the end.

What were Christ's advocacy but a figure and a pretence, had he not given himself an offering for sin? But having died, who shall lay anything to the charge of God's elect?

Christ is a *King.* He rules by the infinite right of his divine nature. "He hath on his vesture and on his thigh a name written, 'King of kings and Lord of lords.'" "All things were created by him and for him." Satan is subject to his control. He has "the keys of death and hell."

But over the *holy* in heaven and earth he rules by *acknowledged* right, and preëminently over the *redeemed*. In their *hearts* has he set up his throne, there to reign without a rival, winning to himself their most ardent affections and profoundest homage.

But what is it that so draws toward him loving and adoring hearts? *He passed to his throne through Calvary.* It is for the crown of thorns and the purple robe and the vesture dyed in blood that his ransomed people crown him Lord of all. These form the golden chain of love which draw and bind them to his throne. In the King upon his holy hill they see the Lamb that was slain; beneath his royal robes they see the mark of the spear; and among his many crowns, one that outshines all the rest and makes them more radiant, — the crown that was meant for shame, but which love has transfigured into a diadem of glory.

"The saints proclaim thee King, and in their hearts
Thy title is engraven with a pen
Dipped in the fountain of eternal love."

Christ shall be *Judge*. He shall sit upon the throne of judgment, and before him shall be gathered all nations. He is "the judge of quick and dead." "All judgment is committed unto the Son."

But whence come his peculiar qualifications for this solemn office? Aside from his divine nature by which he is omniscient and omnipotent, there is a singular fitness in *his* being the arbiter of the destinies of men who, as Son of man, is so identified with our common humanity, and who has given so clear and touching a demonstration of his infinite impartiality. While, on the one hand, as the Son of God, he will see that the authority of Jehovah suffers no detriment; so, on the other, as Son of man, he may be presumed to deal with the utmost fairness and with all possible favor with the race of Adam, among whom he reckons himself after the flesh,—himself the second Adam.

But what consideration, most of all, shall give a fitness and a glory to this office of Christ, to the heart of the believer? It is that he who shall judge him bore not only the same human nature with himself, and was preëminently one with him, "bone of his bone and flesh of his flesh" by a spiritual union; but also,—oh, affecting thought!

inspiring unwavering confidence and exultant hope, —*that he died for him*. How can he who believes in Christ as his Saviour, his Elder Brother, his Advocate, tremble in view of the judgment? If, in deep humility, in conscious personal unworthiness, yet in profound trust and simple love, he can point to the blood of the Lamb covering his sins, will not the Judge acknowledge as a valid plea that which had formed the efficacious ground of his own advocacy for this very believer now standing before him, his younger brother, and pronounce him righteous and bid him welcome? Will not he who is Judge, and also Redeemer and Advocate, sanction his own sacrifice and his own intercessions?

Christ is *the chief attraction of heaven*. It was the farewell promise of Christ to his disciples, " I will come again and receive you unto myself; that where I am, there ye may be also." To the dying thief he said, " This day shalt thou be with me in Paradise." And so an ancient believer said, " I would rather depart and be with Christ;" and another, in a dying hour, " being full of the Holy Ghost, looked up steadfastly into heaven, and saw the glory of God, and Jesus standing on the right hand of God." " Lord Jesus, receive my spirit," was a prayer that showed what was the chief object of his love, and the anticipated source and centre of his heavenly joy. A dying believer of the modern church exclaimed, "I do so long to be with Christ that I could be content to be put to the most exquisite tortures, so I might die and be with Christ." So have believers in all ages felt that to be with Christ would be the answer of their prayers, the fulfilment of their hopes, the end of their faith, and the fulness of their love.

We are told of a mountain of loadstone which could attract ships at a great distance. Nearer and nearer were they brought by an invisible influence and with ever-increasing velocity, until nail after nail was drawn out, when the ship would drop to pieces. So is Christ in heaven ever drawing believers nearer to himself by the powerful magnetism of his love, until, one after another, the cords of their earthly tabernacle shall be loosed, and their freed spirits shall soar aloft to be with "the King in his beauty."

But what gives such edge to these sacred longings to be with Christ? In Christ, God is manifested in a gloried humanity, and a humanity that bears the traces of Calvary's agony.

May, then, the hour of Communion be a time when thy death, O Christ, shall be remembered! While I think of thy life of love, may my reliance for eternal life be upon thine atoning sacrifice! "God forbid that I should glory, save in the cross of our Lord Jesus Christ!"

O SILENT LAMB! for me thou hast endured, —
  Jesus, thou holy, perfect, sinless One!
Thy grief and bitter anguish have secured
    My soul's salvation, when this race is run.
      Then let me, to thine image true,
Thus meekly suffer, with the crown in view.

The narrow way that leads us up to heaven
  Must here through strife and tribulation lie;
Then on the thorny path may strength be given
    This sinful flesh, O Lord, to crucify.
      Oh, take this feebleness away,
And make me strong to bear each future day!

Here daily crosses come to try our weakness,
  Here every member must some burden bear;
But, O my Saviour, if I take with meekness
    The cross appointed by thy love and care,
      Too great, too long, it will not be,
For it is weighed and measured out by thee.

If thus we journey patiently through sadness,
  Each grief will make us dearer to our Lord;
But if we flee the cross in search of gladness,
  We cannot shun his dread avenging sword.
    Oh, blessed they who hear the call,
Who take the cross and follow, leaving all.
            Hymns from the Land of Luther.

O THOU, the contrite sinner's Friend!
Who, loving, lov'st them to the end,
On this alone my hopes depend,
    That thou wilt plead for me.

When, weary in the Christian race,
Far off appears my resting-place,
And, fainting, I mistrust thy grace,
    Then, Saviour, plead for me.

When I have erred and gone astray,
Afar from thine and wisdom's way,
And see no glimmering, guiding ray,
    Still, Saviour, plead for me.

When Satan, by my sins made bold,
Strives from thy cross to loose my hold,
Then with thy pitying arms enfold,
    And plead, oh, plead for me!

And when my dying hour draws near,
Darkened with anguish, guilt, and fear,
Then to my fainting sight appear,
　　Pleading in heaven for me.

When the full light of heavenly day
Reveals my sins in dread array,
Say thou hast washed them all away;
　　Oh, say thou plead'st for me!

CHAPTER X.

CHRIST OUR LIFE — THE NATURE AND EFFECTS OF SPIRITUAL LIFE — PRESIDENT EDWARDS AND HIS WIFE — THE RELATION OF THE SUPPER TO THE CHRISTIAN LIFE — POETRY.

"I am . . . . . the Life. — John 14 : 6.

CHRIST OUR LIFE, — this is the only perfect expression of the fact of spiritual life. However we may attempt to define it, to explain it, to unfold it, to seek other modes of announcing it, we are brought back to the simple inspired statement, feeling that the Christian experience alone can adequately interpret it. The believer's life is "hid with Christ in God." Christ is its hidden spring, whence it issues and derives its perpetual support.

No one Christian has entered into the full comprehension and appropriation of the fact, and therefore there is no disciple who may not be helped in some point by every other disciple. By such mutual comparison of inward experiences, it may be better understood how Christ is our life. If the Spirit of truth assist us, we may hope to shed some light upon a subject so full of interest and importance to every believer, as the inward manifestation of Christ.

Christ is our life as the revealer of life. He is our life as having offered up his life a ransom, in his objective work of redemption, outside of us, upon the cross.

But in another and deeper sense, he is our life, by "*entering into the heart and giving it life.*" It is his taking possession of the inner man, and dwelling there, by his Spirit.

It is of course very inadequately expressed by saying that this inward manifesting of himself to his friends as he does not to the world, is "his manifesting what is divine in his doctrine, his person, and his life; causing it to be perceived, comprehended, and felt."[1] Even this view is too external. It does not satisfy the strong language of Scripture nor the facts of Christian experience. It places Christ too much outside the

[1] *Walker's Sermons.*

soul, and represents him as exerting from without an influence within, instead of his entering into the soul and uniting himself with it as its life.

This life is not a mere imitation of Christ by the simple exercise of the human will striving to be like him, to reproduce his character; not even as aided in this effort by a divine influence; nor is it the mere " restoration of a disarranged constitution."

It is a new spiritual creation, the awakening of a new and higher life, by the indwelling Christ, who is Life in its infinite fulness; it is Christ uniting himself with, and working in and through, the soul, inspiring it with sacred longings, enstamping upon it his own image, and leading it on in a loving imitation of his own example. It is the result of nothing less than " the union of the human spirit with the divine."

It is profoundly interior, seated in the deepest, most permanent, and most susceptible elements of our nature, in the still depths which are " hid from the eyes of all living," — " hid with Christ in God."

When Paul says, " Not I, but Christ liveth in me," he speaks not the language of dreamy mysticism, but of actual experience. It is Christ's living presence in the soul, "Christ in us the hope of glory." It involves a fellowship and inter-communion between Christ and the believer most intimate and abiding, a life that is divine and inextinguishable.

This life in Christ is a fact so wonderful, so sublime, so past all finite comprehension, so fraught with unutterable and infinite and endless blessing, that it has sometimes revealed itself in rapturous joy, in intense longings to be more closely identified with and swallowed up in Christ, to be perfectly conformed to his image, to be entirely obedient to his will, to be adorned with all the graces of his Spirit, to reflect ever and only the light and glory of an indwelling Christ.

"It has often appeared to me delightful," wrote President Edwards, "to be united to Christ; to have him for my Head, and to be a member of his body; also to have Christ for my Teacher and Prophet. I very often think, with longings and pantings of soul, of being a little child, taking hold of Christ, to be led by him through the wilderness of this world. . . . . His blood and atonement have appeared precious, and his righteousness precious, which was always accompanied with ardency of spirit, and inward strugglings and breathings and groanings that cannot be uttered, to be emptied of myself and swallowed up in Christ. . . . Once . . I felt an ardency of soul to be — what I know not otherwise how to express — emptied and annihilated; to lie in the dust, and to be full of Christ alone; to love him with a holy and pure love; to trust in him; to live upon him; to serve and follow him, and to be perfectly sanctified and made pure, with a divine and heavenly purity."

His eminently gifted and godly wife had an extraordinary experience, at one time, of the power and depth of this life, giving us an idea of its expansion in all the elements of inexpressible purity and bliss in the heavenly world.

"All night," she wrote, "I continued in a constant, clear, and lively sense of the heavenly sweetness of Christ's excellent and transcendent love, of his nearness to me, and of my nearness to him, with an inexpressibly sweet calmness of soul in an entire rest in him. I seemed to myself to perceive a flow of divine love come down from the heart of Christ in heaven into my heart, in a constant flowing and reflowing of heavenly and divine love from Christ's heart to mine; and I appeared to myself to float or swim in these bright, sweet beams of the love of Christ, like the motes swimming in the beams of the sun."

But this life in Christ, though susceptible of such elevation and even ecstacy, is not to be regarded as chiefly consisting in outgushes of joy, nor, especially, as fairly represented by an ascetic quietism. It is generally, and, in our present state of existence, most fittingly, characterized by a calmer flow, as it manifests itself amid the common affairs of our ordinary life. It was never designed to be an exceptional or occasional experience, for a favored few, but to be the distinctive privilege of all God's children. It is this which constitutes them children.

While, then, it may sometimes bear the Christian on the wings of faith up the lofty heights of devotion and rapt communion with Christ, making the world to sink into nothingness in the sublime ascent, and the soul to lose itself in wonder and praise and love, yet, at present, it chiefly delights to lead him along the common paths of Christian duty, and to inspire him with courage amid the hard conflicts which form so large a part of his earthly experience. It has equally to do with the loftiest devotion and the homeliest duty. It is for the closet and the counting-room,[1] for the Sabbath and the week-day, for the pulpit and the parlor, the workshop[2] or the kitchen. It is the breathing forth of holy desires, and the inspiration of deeds of charity. It is prayer, praise, joy; it is penitence, confession, the peace of pardon; it is faith, hope, and love; it is patience, meekness, trust; it is the aiming, in every place and at all times, to be and to do all that Christ approves; it prompts the fervent prayer for the conversion of sinners;

---

[1] That well-known and most truly Christian merchant, Nath. R. Cobb, once remarked to his pastor, "I think I can say that my aim in making money is the same as that of every true minister of Christ in preaching the gospel."

It was so most eminently with that merchant-prince of England, John Thornton, whose life and business talents and immense fortune were consecrated to Christ. Samuel Budgett was another example, the successful head of a "Christian mercantile establishment," a "real, earnest Christian," living "as if in the continual sense of having been made by Christ one of God's high priests upon earth," and as such having a daily and tender solicitude for the religious welfare of all who were in his employ.

[2] "Bernard Palissy is the most perfect model of the workman." — *Lamartine.*

"He is the patriarch of the workshop, showing how to exalt and ennoble any business, however trivial, so that it has labor for its means, progress and beauty for its motive, and the glory of God for its end." "I have not been willing," said he, "to hide in the ground those talents it has pleased God to allot me, but to cause them to yield profit and increase to him from whom I have received them." His was truly a Christian life.

it breathes the heartfelt exhortation; it starts the tear of pity over the wayward and lost.

Christ can allow no rival power, not even in the smallest point. The Christian is not authorized to take excursions into outside regions to gratify self, whence he may return to pay his homage to Jesus. Christ claims the right of being his perpetual companion and guide, to go and return with him, to be his indwelling spirit, seeking to make his whole life harmonious with the will of God, exalting even its commonest duties into heavenly ministrations, through the sacred motive that inspires them; so that in whatsoever place or work, Christ will shine out and be glorified.

"I live no longer *myself*," — my old self,[1] — wrote one who was an illustrious example of this spiritual life in Christ, — " but Christ that liveth in me. And the life that I now live in the flesh, I live by the faith of the Son of God, who loved me and gave himself for me." This covers the whole ground of conscious existence and activity.

"Each believer has his life in Christ; its root is spiritual fellowship with him. To be a Christian and to be in Christ, to be in fellowship with him and to live, are one and the same thing. Christ

---

[1] Ellicott's rendering.

himself is the vital principle from which all proceeds. Out of him unfolds itself the entire new life."[1] The soul has spiritual life only as Christ lives in it.

The Lord's Supper has been ordained as a means of grace, for the renewal of this life, for confirming our fellowship with Christ our Life, for reminding us of his infinite love; so that from this memorial scene the believer may go forth to his earthly cares and duties, to live out more perfectly the life of Christ; to show how completely adapted is that life to meet every duty and beautify every sphere of human existence. Christ our Life! blessed and glorious truth! the Infinite dwelling in the finite, and communicating to it of its own inexhaustible fulness, lifting the soul that was once dead in sin up to the fellowship and likeness of the Highest and Best.

Mighty Power! so penetrating, controlling, transforming! What is its secret?

As we seek an answer to this question, we are soon brought to the Cross. An irresistible attraction draws us thither. There is the "hiding" of the Redeemer's "power." All the infinite wisdom, holiness, and benignity of Heaven there glow

---

[1] Neander. *First Epistle of John*, p. 66.

with a radiance surpassing the lustre of ten thousand suns. All the considerations which can most powerfully influence and transform human hearts, meet at that sacred spot. There especially beams out infinite mercy. And therefore the cross is the place of Christ's coronation as Lord and Life of the believing soul. It is because Christ was crucified that he is our Life, and that we most fully believe that he has an unquestionable right to guide and mould us according to his will and into his own image.

There can be no true, loyal life but in *liberty;* and Christ, by his death upon the cross, confers the "freedom of the sons of God" upon them that believe. They are free from guilt and condemnation and fear; they have conscious peace with God, and therefore the spirit of children. "The spirit of life in Christ Jesus" causes new life to pervade the whole inner man.

Love is Life in its highest form,

"In *His* unerring sight, who measures life by Love;"

for "God is Love," and Christ the most perfect manifestation of that fundamental aspect of the divine nature. It is this sublime life, flowing out

of love, of which Paul speaks when he describes Christ as living in him, and Christ as his life:—
" The love of Christ constraineth us, because we thus judge, that if one died for all, then were all dead; and that he died for all, that they who live should not henceforth live unto themselves, but unto him *who died for them*, and rose again. . . . . Therefore if any man be in Christ, he is a new creature;" his whole inner spirit is changed; Christ is the inspiration and end of his being. "Through all times, through eternity," wrote one, " has my spirit, restless, wandered; but nothing seized my whole heart until I came to Golgotha,— to God be all the praise!"

The Lord's Supper also indicates to us that Christ is the perpetual *sustenance* and *support* of this Life. His own words, in the sixth chapter of John, though not directly referring to this ordinance are yet strikingly suggestive of it, and are interpreted by the believing and loving heart as showing that holy and blessed spiritual union which exists between Christ and those who receive him by faith, and which constitutes the ground of this Life and the means of its perpetuation and perfection. "I am the *Living Bread* which came down from heaven: if any man eat of this bread he shall live forever, and the bread that I will give him is my flesh, which I will give for the life of the world. . . . Whoso eateth my flesh, and drinketh my blood, hath eternal life. . . . . He that eateth my flesh and drinketh my blood, dwelleth in me and I in him."[1]

The Lord's Supper reminds us of our constant and supreme dependence on Christ for spiritual life. To change the figure, preserving the idea, we are taught to "*abide*" in Christ that we may bring forth fruit. "Union with Christ,— this is the secret of all fruitfulness. . . . We abide in him by acts of earnest and constant prayer, by the study and devout meditation of his Holy Word, by meeting him often in the communion of his holy sacrament; even as, in respect of this last means of abiding, it is very noticeable that these words about the vine and vine-branches, — this 'abide in me and I in you,' — follows im-

---

[1] "He here speaks of the participation of divine life by means of his appearance in humanity, of the impartation of divine life depending upon and accomplished by the historical Christ, while he guards himself against being supposed to speak of his body in a literal sense, by giving us a key for the right interpretation of his words. 'The Spirit giveth life—the flesh profiteth nothing.'"— *Neander, Planting and Training of the Christian Church*, p. 321.

mediately in time on the institution of the sacrament of union, the festival of Christ's blessed body and blood. And so shall he abide in you."[1]

How true and free and beautiful is this Life in Christ, the result of his indwelling by the Spirit, Christ inciting to duty, restraining from evil, regulating the passions, subduing pride, enlarging the heart, and conforming the whole man to his own glorious image. Glorious in its earthly beginnings, what must it be in its heavenly perfection? Profoundly mysterious, yet so simple, so natural, so consonant with our free activity, that the man in whom Christ dwells, whose life Christ most effectually controls, whose life *is* Christ, is only more truly man, more nobly himself.

Blessed Saviour! bless to us our participation of the emblems of thy death. May we spiritually eat and drink. May our spiritual life be nourished and strengthened. May we grow up into thee, our living Head. May ours be the resolution of the sainted Boardman,—" Till we get [to heaven], let us build us a little tabernacle close by the cross of Calvary, and watch our Saviour, and hear what he will say: "*Ye are dead, and your life is hid with Christ in God.*'" May our will so blend with

[1] *Trench's Sermons*, p. 108.

thine, O perfect One, that we shall have no separate wish, walking in that liberty wherewith thou makest thy people free.

That mystic word of thine, O sovereign Lord,
  Is all too pure, too high, too deep for me;
Weary with striving, and with longing faint,
  I breathe it back again in prayer to thee.

Abide in me, I pray, and I in thee;
  From this good hour, oh, leave me nevermore;
Then shall the discord cease, the wound be healed,
  The life-long bleeding of the soul be o'er.

Abide in me; o'ershadow by thy love
  Each half-formed purpose, and dark thought of sin;
Quench, e'er it rise, each selfish, low desire,
  And keep my soul, as thine, calm and divine.

As some rare perfume, in a vase of clay,
  Pervades it with a fragrance not its own;
So, when thou dwellest in a mortal soul,
  All heaven's own sweetness seems around it thrown.

The soul alone, like a neglected harp,
   Grows out of tune, and needs that hand divine;
Dwell thou within it, tune and touch the chords,
   Till every note and string shall answer thine.

Abide in me; there have been moments pure,
   When I have seen thy face and felt thy power;
Then evil lost its grasp, and passion, hushed,
   Owned the divine enchantments of the hour.

These were but seasons beautiful and rare;
   Abide in me, and they shall ever be:
I pray thee now fulfil my earnest prayer,
   Come and abide in me, and I in thee.

H. B. STOWE.

If thou, true Life, wilt in me live,
   Consume whate'er is not of thee:
One look of thine more joy can give
   Than all the world can offer me.
O Jesus, be thou mine forever,
Nought from thy love my heart can sever,
As thou has promised in thy Word;
   Oh, deep the joy whereof I drink
   Whene'er my soul in thee can sink,
And own her Bridegroom and her Lord!

O Heart, that glowed with love and died,
   Kindle my soul with fire divine;
Lord, in the heart thou'st won, abide,
   And all in it that is not thine
Oh let me conquer and destroy,
Strong in thy love, thou fount of joy.
Nay, be thou conqueror, Lord, in me.
   So shall I triumph o'er despair,
   O'er death itself thy victory share,
Thus suffer, live, and die in thee.

Lead, Saviour, lead, amid the encircling gloom,
     Lead thou me on.
The night is dark, and I am far from home,
     Lead thou me on.
Keep thou my feet; I do not ask to see
The distant scene, — one step's enough for me.

I was not ever thus, nor prayed that thou
     Shouldst lead me on;
I loved to choose and see my path; but now
     Lead thou me on.
I loved the glare of day, and, spite of fears,
Pride ruled my will; remember not past years.

So long thy power hath blessed me, — sure, it still
    Will lead me on
O'er vale and hill, through stream and torrent, till
    The night is gone;
And with the morn those angel faces smile,
Which I have loved long since, and lost awhile.

O Lamp of Life! that on the bloody cross
  Dost hang, the Beacon of our wandering race,
  To guide us homeward to our resting-place,
And save our best wealth from eternal loss!
To purge my inward sight from earthly dross
  That fixed upon thy cross, or near or far,
In all the storms this weary bark that toss,
  (Whate'er be lost in that tempestuous war,)
  Thee I retain, my Compass and my Star!
That, when arrived upon the wished-for strand,
  I pass of death th' irrevocable bar,
And at the gate of heaven, trembling, stand,
  The everlasting doors may open wide,
  And give thee to my sight, God glorified!
Charles Dyson.

CHAPTER XI.

CHRIST A SUFFERER — CONSOLATION FOR THE AFFLICTED — THE DISCIPLINE OF SORROW — FELLOWSHIP WITH CHRIST — THE DEATH OF CHRIST AS RELATED TO AFFLICTION.

"Surely he hath borne our griefs and carried our sorrows."
Isaiah 53: 4.

THE CHURCH UNDER THE CROSS, — so did the Reformed Church of Holland style itself in the days of its early weakness and persecution. Days of trial and sorrow they were, but of purity and spiritual growth.

"From the day when Jesus Christ purchased us upon a cross, all that is great, powerful, healthful, is tinged with sadness; and all the seeds of life and regeneration are sown in sorrow and death."[1]

There is something almost sacred in sorrow.

[1] Adolphe Monod. *Discourses on St. Paul.*

"It is a relic of Christ in the world; an image of the great Sufferer; a shadow of the cross."[1]

> "The holy name of Grief; holy herein,
> That by the grief of ONE came all our good."[2]

How noble its discipline, how valuable its lessons, when the Divine Spirit uses it in the exercise of his great office as Enlightener, Comforter, and Sanctifier. Then it is no longer the "sorrow of the world, which worketh death," but that "godly sorrow which is unto life." Then shall it be found true, that, though "weeping may endure for a night, joy cometh in the morning."

The heart that has never felt the "furnace-heat" of a great affliction has paid dear for its exemption. Its faith may be genuine, but it lacks that quality of calm and steadfast assurance which belongs to the faith that has been shaken by the tempest, and made to strike its roots deeper into the promises of God. Its love may be sincere, but it lacks that simple purity and all-embracing tenderness which comes of sanctified affliction. Its joys may be real and many, but they are superficial when compared with that bliss which he enjoys who, in the time of supreme need, has

[1] W. Archer Butler. *Sermons.*   [2] Mrs. Browning.

experienced the exceeding preciousness of the promises; who, through his tears, has beheld his Saviour nearer and dearer than ever, and heaven also nearer and more glorious. His smiles are "glory-beaming," the revelation of a profound and satisfying consciousness of having passed beyond the "broken cisterns," and drank at the ever-flowing fountain of truth and gladness. "Blessed are they that mourn, for they shall be comforted."

Trials may be attended with sad and startling revelations of self, with the blighting of hopes, the breaking of idols, the staining of pride, the bowing of the soul in the very dust; but the sense of want and helplessness may beget the cry for mercy,— a cry never unheard in heaven,— and so out of weakness may come strength, and out of darkness light, out of dismay,

"———— the peace which floweth as a river;"

and the heart become the richer in all the fruits of love, and life assume a new seriousness and grandeur. Thus the slave of passion may be transformed into an angel of mercy; and the Christian whose heart had been "divided," and his ways unstable, and his character sadly incomplete and unsymmetrical, into a pattern of humility and devotion.

"One of the richest mines in the world was accidently discovered by a peasant, as he was slowly climbing up a difficult steep. He caught at a bush to save himself and steady his steps; the bush gave way, but disclosed at the same time the exhaustless treasure which lay concealed underneath." So, in the stern struggle of life, or toiling up some difficult ascent, amid trial and sorrow, we, almost in our desperation, grasp at many supports, only to have them fail us; yet then it is that the hitherto hidden power of faith in the unseen Redeemer is revealed, giving unwonted energy to the soul, and a new discovery of the unsearchable riches of his grace.

Sometimes trials seem to hide us away, apart from men, in the "cleft of the rock," but it is that we may see the glory of Jehovah passing by. There, shut out from the world and up to ourselves and God, faith gains new clearness of vision, becomes far-sighted, or brings the distant near.

"I have often," says Ruskin, "seen the summit of a snowy mountain look nearer than its base, owing to the perfect clearness of the upper sky." So, sometimes, in affliction's hour, when all around is dark, heaven's mountain-tops seem nearer than the earth, Christ closer to us and more distinctly visible than the dearest friend by our side and in our sight; for faith, refined by suffering, makes the upper realm — the Redeemer's home — to shine with unwonted clearness. To the eye of Stephen, Christ was nearer than his murderers, nearer than his brethren that stood around him. The mists might rest upon the foot of the mountain, but all was clear above, so as he had never seen it till this the hour of his martyrdom.

> "———— Thou canst not tell
> How rich a dowry sorrow gives thy soul,
> How firm a faith, and eagle sight of God."

Let us listen to a passage from the experience of the author of *Token for Mourners*,[1] — author and work both of blessed memory: "I know, says one, no man hath a velvet cross, but the cross is made of what God will have it; yet I dare not say, Oh, that I had liberty to sell Christ's cross, lest therewith also I should sell joy, comfort, sense of love, patience, and the kind visits of the Bridegroom. I have but small experience of sufferings for Christ; but I find a young heaven, and a little

---
[1] Flavel.

paradise of glorious comforts, and soul-delighting visits from Christ, in suffering for him and his truth. My prison is my palace, my sorrow is full of joy, my losses are rich losses, my pain easy pain, my heavy days are holy days and happy days. I may tell a new tale of Christ to my friends. Grace tried is better than grace and more than grace. It is glory in its infancy. Who knows the truth of grace without a trial? And how soon would faith freeze without a cross! Bear your cross, therefore, with joy."

Christian sonship brings, then, no exemption from trial. "Only one Son without sin, but not one without suffering."

But here is our consolation and glory, that Christianity interprets all our sorrows, declaring their sacred ministry, and how they may be turned to joy. It teaches how to "glory in tribulation." It bids us anticipate, as the end of our sorrows, a "far more exceeding and eternal weight of glory."

Above all, the revelation of *Jesus* is the "strong consolation;" and therefore to the Christian mourner the *Lord's Supper* is a most precious ordinance.

It is the memorial of a *Fellow-Sufferer*. The exalted and sinless One was a "Man of sorrows and acquainted with grief." "He was tempted in all points like as we are." He can be "touched with the feeling of our infirmities."

And how full of comfort is the thought that he *chose* to be a Man of sorrows, *on purpose to be our companion in suffering.* Was ever love or sympathy like this?

With a full view of all the grief and anguish involved in his earthly sojourn, he resolved, in the infinite pity of his heart, to make it his personal experience, to take up our sorrows into his bosom and carry them as his own.

"Jesus wept!" What a revelation of heaven's compassion!

> "Call thou on him, for he, in human form,
>   Hath walked the waves of life, and stilled the storm."

But Christ was *no ordinary sufferer.* He made an acquaintance with grief beyond our possible experience. He penetrated its deepest mysteries. He exhausted all the possibilities of woe. Well might he say, "All ye that pass by, behold, and see if there be any sorrow like unto my sorrow." However much we suffer, he more. Our cross is sometimes heavy, but not like the cross of the Redeemer's agony. "The great wave of affliction did first beat on him, and being thereby broken, some small sparks [sprays] of it only do light on us." As we struggle on in the path of trial or temptation, still we see his footprints ever in advance.

Surely the thought that he, the innocent Lamb of God, was yet so great a sufferer, — far, far beyond our possible experience of trial, — must tend to check our murmurs, and make us patient and submissive. Oh, what but trifles *are* our heaviest sorrows, when compared with his?

Suffering one! are you *poor?* Not as the "houseless wanderer of Galilee," who "had not where to lay his head," who "for our sakes became poor that we through his poverty might become rich." Are you *reproached* and *slighted*, your name cast out as evil? Not as he who was "despised and rejected of men," whose unsullied purity could not save him from the basest calumnies, as a man of low tastes and degrading friendships, a slave to appetite, a disturber of society, a hypocrite, a blasphemer, an imposter, a confederate of Satan. Are you *tempted?* Not as he who was "led up of the Spirit into the wilderness to be tempted of the devil," given up as it were to the wiliest arts and most malicious assaults of Satan.

Are you even *a slave*, suffering from cruel stripes? Did not Jesus become a "servant"? was he not bound and scourged and crucified, like the vilest slave and malefactor? and is it not "by his stripes we are healed"? Have you *trials and perplexities in the business of life?* Is the path of duty often rough and unpleasant? Do human weakness and imperfection and sin mar and sadden the intercourse between man and man, even among friends and brethren? Ah, who can tell how much Jesus suffered from the instability of human friendship, from ingratitude and prejudice, from envy and insolence and malice? Who can estimate the violence done to his pure and delicate spirit, so attuned to all that is good and true and noble, by his long residence among the rude and rebellious, by the treatment he received, in his last and saddest hours, from his own disciples, when not one of them could watch with him even one hour, when one long-professed friend betrayed him, another real but timid one denied him, and all at length forsook him and fled, leaving him alone to die? Have you *trials of the spirit*, sorer than all possible outward calamities? What human experience can begin to measure the griefs of the Saviour's soul, when he "groaned in spirit," when he "offered up prayers and supplications, with strong crying and tears," when he was "sore amazed and very heavy," when he said, "My soul is exceeding sorrowful unto death," and when he cried out from the cross, "My God! my God! why hast thou forsaken me?" Whose Gethsemane can be like his? Into the strange mystery of his desolation upon Calvary, who can penetrate? The bloody sweat, the breaking heart, the fearful forsaking, are all his own.

And yet this mighty sufferer was the Son of man, — our Brother!

Oh, never did a heart beat so intensely human as his, so profoundly in sympathy with our suffering, sorrowing humanity. With a most delicate and tender appreciation of human want and of the yearning of the soul for sympathy, he can enter into the case of every one that seeks his help. And never shall one say that Christ failed to understand or meet his want, that his friendship disappointed him and made him feel that, after all, he must turn elsewhere for relief. He was our Brother in trial, and is our Brother in sympathy. We may "come boldly unto the throne of grace, to obtain mercy and find grace to help in time of need." " In that he himself hath suffered, being tempted, he *is* able to succor them that are tempted."

A popular writer of our country[1] says of one who was passing through a great sorrow: — " She could speak to no one, — not to her mother, nor to her spiritual guide, — for had she not passed to a region beyond theirs? As well might those on the hither side of mortality instruct the souls gone beyond the veil, as souls outside a great affliction guide those who are struggling in it. *That is a mighty baptism, and only Christ can go down with us into those waters.*"

To a sick friend, Dr. Arnold wrote: "I have been led to think, from time to time, what would be my greatest support and comfort, if it should please God to visit me either with a very painful or a very dangerous illness; and I have always thought that, in both, nothing would do me so much good as to read, over and over again, the account of the sufferings and death of Christ, as given in the different gospels. For if it be a painful complaint, we shall find that in mere pain he suffered most severely, and in a great variety of ways; and, if it be a dangerous complaint, then we shall see that Christ suffered very greatly from

[1] Mrs. Stowe.

the fear of death, and was very sorely troubled in his mind up to the time almost of his actually dying. And one great reason why he bore all this was that we might be supported and comforted when we have to bear the same." [1]

These testimonials of Christ as our Burden-bearer might be multiplied a thousand-fold. In the highest and humblest walks of life, he has performed and still performs this ministry of love and consolation.

"Come [then] and see the victories of the cross. Christ's wounds are thy healing, his agonies thy repose, his conflicts thy conquests, his groans thy songs, his pains thine ease, his death thy life, his sufferings thy salvation."

But there is a *deeper connection* between our suffering and the suffering of Christ. He is to us not merely a companion in trial, and a comforter. He is presented to us in a far higher view, as the glorious *Pattern,* into whose likeness we are to be changed. This is the grand consummation of the Christian's hopes, — to be like his Redeemer.

Here comes in the most sacred ministry of suffering. We are carried out of ourselves, beyond our personal consolation, to the far nobler and

---

[1] *Life and Correspondence.*

more disinterested end of a perfect character. We are to be made "*perfect* through suffering,"—*like unto Christ* by *suffering with Christ*. "That I may know him," was the exultant declaration of an Apostle, "and the power of his resurrection, and the fellowship of his sufferings, being made conformable unto his death." Not but that there were peculiar features and depths in Christ's sufferings as sacrificial and atoning,—the "holy of holies of his passion," into whose sacred mysteries the finite can never pass. But there is a certain length to which we can go with Christ as the "Man of sorrows," and it is only as we thus descend with him into the valley and share his sufferings, thus "drink of the cup that he drank of, and be baptized with the baptism that he was baptized with," that we can enter into the closest and tenderest communion with him, and be completely assimmilated to him. "To suffer together creates a dearer fellow-feeling than to labor together. Companionship in sorrow forms the most enduring of ties; afflicted hearts cling to and grow into each other."[1] "*Pain is the deepest thing we have in our nature*, and union through pain has always seemed more real and more holy than any other."[2]

[1] Eadie. *Com. on Phil.* [2] Arthur Hallam.

Says Spurgeon, "We can never so well see the color of Christ's love as in the night of weeping. .... No revelation of Christ is so truly a revelation as that which is seen in the Patmos of suffering." Thus do we penetrate into the deep and most blessed mystery of the brotherhood of Christ.

Suffering with Christ is a wide and profound theme, full of interest to every disciple. In an important sense, *all* the trial of the Christian is a suffering with Christ, inasmuch as he is one with Christ, a member of his mystical body, and the Head sympathizes with every part. Christ's sympathizing presence is never wanting, even when the dark cloud hides his face for a time. In this sense, the disciple can never suffer without Christ.

He is with us in all our affliction, because it is through this that he is perpetually carrying forward his great purpose of conforming us to his image. Even in our ordinary trials, we suffer with Christ, when we seek to bear them and to improve them in his strength, leaning upon his arm, trusting in his grace.

But there is suffering which is *specially* a "fellowship with the sufferings of Christ," and that is when it is with immediate and purposed reference to his kingdom and glory, as when Paul died daily, "always bearing about the dying of the Lord Jesus," coveting and glorying in affliction and even death out of love to his blessed Master. The noble company of martyrs were eminent examples of suffering with Christ, counting not their lives dear unto them, so that in life or death Christ might be magnified. Multitudes in lowly walks have known the fellowship of Christ's sufferings, amid sacrifices, privations, hardships, perhaps petty but perpetual annoyances, or harsh reproaches from ungodly relatives. Meekly, perhaps in solitude, bearing their daily cross after Christ, because his truth and his Person were dearer than all else, they were true martyrs, suffering with Christ, and so becoming more Christlike.

There is a yet *deeper sense* in which we may suffer with Christ, be more truly baptized with his baptism. His great work was consummated in the garden and on the cross. There he endured his deepest and most peculiar woes, those which most clearly illustrated his character, and most effectually accomplished the purpose of his mission. There he went down into the deepest waters. In Olivet and on Calvary the burden of a world's sins lay upon his soul; he was in the pains of travail for a "a new creation." In the darkness of the garden, a deeper shadow fell upon his spirit as the sins of men would seem to have become almost the subject of personal consciousness, taken up, as it were, into his own soul, while he, the Substitute of the guilty, untainted by their sins, yet felt with the keenest and most agonizing sensitiveness their foulness and bitterness, and unutterable and infinite misery, and struggled in the birth-throes of a great Deliverance.

Can we go with Christ down into those mysterious depths? Is there for us a Gethsemane and a Calvary? Can we be "crucified with Christ?" If we are one with Christ, if we can know the fellowship of his sufferings, may it not be possible to know something of these deepest and most unselfish griefs of our Redeemer? Is it not so with the Christian when he "travails in birth, until Christ be formed in" the hearts of the sinful and lost, when his soul almost breaks beneath the burden of other's sins, and, as if his soul were in their souls' place and were itself exposed to the "curse" which threatens them, he bears these lost and loved ones, perhaps "bone of his bone, and flesh of his flesh," up to the sympathies of the great

Burden-bearer, pleading with " strong crying and tears" for their eternal life ?[1]

Does he not thus gain a deeper understanding of the mystery of Christ's Passion? While his faith is strengthened in the feeling that Christ can understand and sympathize with his soul's most agonized pleadings, and thus he is encouraged to labor for the salvation of the lost, does he not gain more precious views of Christ? does he not feel a profounder gratitude to so great a Friend? is he not drawn to him with a stronger violence of desire to be with him and like him? Oh, the glory and preciousness of a Being who

---

[1] " There is one particular kind of exercise and concern of mind that many have been overpowered by, ... and that is the deep concern and distress that they have been in *for the souls of others.* . . . Why should it be thought strange that those that are full of the spirit of Christ should be proportionably, in their love to souls, like Christ? who had so strong a love and concern for them as to be willing to drink the dregs of the cup of God's fury for them; and at the same time that he offered up his blood for souls, offered up also, as their High Priest, strong crying and tears, with an extreme agony, wherein the soul of Christ was as it were in travail for the souls of the elect; and therefore in saving them he is said to see of the *travail* of his soul.

"As such a spirit of love to and concern for souls was the spirit of Christ, so is it the spirit of the church; and therefore the Church, in desiring and seeking that Christ might be brought forth in the world and in the souls of men, is represented (Rev. 12) as a 'woman crying, travailing in birth, and pained to be delivered."—*Jonathan Edwards, Thoughts on the Revival in New England,* 1740.

descended from such a height to such amazing depths of sorrow and anguish, to save his enemies!

May there not be a yet *further* "fellowship with the sufferings of Christ" *in the hidings of his Father's face?* Always is Christ alone and preëminent, here as elsewhere; and yet the disciple may be drawn within the outer shadows, while his Master goes "yonder" into the deeper gloom. Who shall say that that feeling of darkness and doubt and desolation which sometimes comes over the Christian heart, when the hold upon earth and heaven seems to be gone, may not form a purposed part of genuine Christian experience, designed, perhaps, in some little measure to bring us into "fellowship with the sufferings of Christ" when he was "forsaken," and to furnish a more thorough proof that our salvation depends not upon our feelings, upon our own conscious efforts, upon even our own faith viewed as a personal exercise or act, but alone upon that unseen Arm which we find to be underneath us, even when least we see it. The effect of such an experience, when rightly viewed, is to carry us more entirely out of ourselves, and to make us rest with a more unshaken and joyful confidence upon that foundation which God has laid in Zion, the perfect righteousness of Christ. Finding, when all was dark and drear, when even our God seemed removed to an infinite distance from us, when our own hearts gave back scarcely a response to allay our fears, — that even then we were resting securely in the arms of omnipotent covenant mercy, we come forth of the gloom to walk henceforth in the brighter light of a more assured experience. Having outrode the most stormy billows amid the darkest night, hereafter we learn to commit the whole keeping of our souls to the heavenly Pilot, who had himself passed through and out of a far deeper gloom and more overwhelming billows to the "joy that was set before him." We are taught to sink into Christ's arms, to cease from our own vain endeavors to maintain the Christian walk, to rest in the promised strength of the ever-present, all-sufficient Saviour.

Even spiritual joys are not free from danger. Pride and self-righteousness and self-confidence stand ready to be spoilers of our peace when we come down from "the mount." And therefore our Master must resort to various methods of discipline, to break us into perfect submission, some of them most painful, and some most humiliating. Spiritual desertion, which is not, however, a real abandonment, but only a hiding of our Father's face for a season, may be, in some cases, the only effectual cure of the fast-cleaving tendency of our nature to rest in self, — in frames and feelings and acts of our own. This method is of course designed to effect a profounder self-knowledge and self-abandonment, and a firmer clinging to Christ, and a more stable and joyful resting upon "the foundation." The soul that has truly gone with Christ — even with a Christ for the time unseen — through these deep waters, becomes thereby more identified with Christ, and learns to live more truly the life of faith. It walks now with firmer tread, because, having "no confidence in the flesh," it can glory in the cross of Christ, it can more profoundly adopt as its own the precious words of Holy Writ, " Blessed be the God and Father of our Lord Jesus Christ, which, according to his abundant mercy, hath begotten us again unto a lively hope by the resurrection of Jesus Christ from the dead, to an inheritance incorruptible and undefiled, and that fadeth not away, reserved in heaven for you who *are kept by the power of God* through faith unto salvation ready to be revealed in the last time. Wherein ye greatly rejoice, though now for a season, if need be, ye are in heaviness, through manifold temptations; that the trial of your faith, being much more precious than of gold which perisheth, though it be tried with fire, might be found unto praise and honor and glory at the appearing of Jesus Christ: whom *having not seen* ye love; in whom, though *now ye see him not*, yet believing, ye rejoice with joy unspeakable and full of glory."[1]

Let us then gird up the loins of our minds, and gratefully accept the order of grace, —

"The wholesome ministry of pain."

"What happened to Jesus as Head of the church, must necessarily be partaken of by all his members."[2] "The servant is not greater than his Lord." "Take heaven with the wind on your face," said the saintly Rutherford, "for so both storm and wind were on the fair face of your lovely Forerunner, Christ, all his way." So shall Christ be forming in us, more and more, the "hope of glory." Would we then be "followers of God as dear children"? we must follow the Son, who "learned obedience by the things which he suffered." Would we learn "not to trust in ourselves, but in Him that raiseth the dead?" we must

[1] 1 Peter 1: 3-8. [2] Jacqueline Pascal.

be "pressed out of measure, and despair even of life." "The strength of Christ must be made perfect in weakness." The thorn must penetrate our flesh, even as it pierced his sacred brow, would we know how "sufficient" is that "grace" for us which revealed itself in him in a heavenly patience. Would we at length walk with him in white? we must, as he did, wear the robe of shame and the weeds of woe. Would we drink the new wine in the kingdom of God? we must press to our lips the cup mingled with gall. Would we wear the crown? we must bear the cross. The valley of humiliation, as for Christ so for us, is in the way to the celestial city. The glory of it is, that we follow him.

> "Welcome the thorniest path, if there
> The print-marks of his feet appear;
> If in his footsteps we may tread,
> And follow where our Lord hath led."

Christianity thus converts our sorrows into a sublime discipline, into the means and pledges of a perfect resemblance to Christ, as in moral features so in future bliss. If he suffered and entered into glory, so shall we in him; "for both he that sanctifieth and they who are sanctified, are all of one:

for which cause he is not ashamed to call them brethren."[1]

The DEATH of Christ — that fearful climax of all his sufferings — is the grand explanation and relief of the sufferings of his disciples. That death, as propitiatory and atoning, changes the slaves of of sin and Satan, by the power of the Holy Spirit working faith in the soul, into *the sons of God,* and of consequence *changes their relation to all things,* — to life and death, — and, what we now especially contemplate, to all the events and circumstances of our present existence. "In Christ all things are pleasant and work together for our good. Death is no exception, for Christ suffered and died, that he might sanctify death and sorrow."[2]

At the Cross — and only there — can the believer, "accepted in the Beloved" and heir of all things, say, "I take pleasure in infirmities, in reproaches, in necessities, in persecution, in distresses, for Christ's sake: for when I am weak, then am I strong;" or again, "I reckon that the sufferings of this present time are not worthy to be compared with the glory which shall be revealed in us," even to be "glorified together" with Christ; or

---

[1] Hebrews ii. 11.   [2] Jacqueline Pascal.

yet again, " Our light affliction, which is but for a moment, worketh for us a far more exceeding and eternal weight of glory;"—for the cross assures us, " He that spared not his own Son, but delivered him up for us all, how shall he not with him also freely give us all things?"

There are those who sigh that no fond heart is theirs;
None love them best. Oh, vain and selfish sigh!
Out of the bosom of His love he spares, —
The Father spares the Son, for thee to die.
For thee he died. For thee he lives again;
O'er thee he watches in his boundless reign.

KEBLE.

The way is long and weary,
  The path is bleak and bare;
Our feet are worn and weary,
  But we will not despair.
More heavy was thy burden,
  More desolate thy way;
O Lamb of God, who takest
  The sin of the world away,
    Have mercy on us!

The snows lie thick around us,
  In the dark and gloomy night;
And the tempest wails above us,
  And the stars have hid their light;
But blacker was the darkness
  Round Calvary's cross that day;—
O Lamb of God, who takest
  The sin of the world away,
    Have mercy on us!

Our hearts are faint with sorrow,
  Heavy and hard to bear;
For we dread the bitter morrow,
  But we will not despair;
Thou knowest all our anguish,
  And thou wilt bid it cease;—
O Lamb of God, who takest
  The sin of the world away,
    Have mercy on us!
          ADELAIDE ANN PROCTOR.

GOD draws a cloud over each gleaming morn;
    Would we ask why?
It is because all noblest things are born
    In agony.

Only upon *some cross* of pain or woe
    God's sun may lie;
Each soul, redeemed from self and sin, must know
    Its Calvary.

Yet we must crave neither for joy nor grief;
      God chooses best;
He only knows our sick soul's fit relief,
      And gives us rest.

More than our feeble hearts can ever pine
      For holiness,
That Father, in his tenderness divine,
      Yearneth to bless.

He never sends a joy not meant in love,
      Still less a pain;
Our gratitude the sunlight falls to prove,
      Our faith, the rain.

In his hands we are safe, — we falter on
      Through storm and mire;
Above, beside, around us, there is One
      Will never tire.

What though we fall, and bruised and wounded lie, —
      Our lips in dust;
God's arm shall lift us up to victory;
      In him we trust.

For neither life, nor death, nor things below,
      Nor things above.
Shall ever sever us that we should go
      From this great love.

If God compel thee to this destiny,—
  To *die alone*, with none beside thy bed
To ruffle round with sobs thy last word said,
  And mark with tears the pulses ebb from thee,
Pray then alone,—" O Christ, come tenderly!
  By thy forsaken Sonship in the red
Dread wine-press; by the wilderness outspread,
  And the lone garden, where thine agony
Fell bloody from thy brow,—by all of those
  Permitted desolations, comfort mine!
No earthly friend being near me, interpose
  No deathly angel 'twixt my face and thine;
But stoop thyself to gather my life's rose,
  And smile away my mortal to divine."

MRS. BROWNING. *Sonnets.*

He knelt, the Saviour knelt and prayed,
  When but his Father's eye
Looked through the lonely garden's shade
  On that dread agony;
The Lord of all above, beneath,
Was bowed with sorrow unto death.

The sun set in a fearful hour,
  The stars might well grow dim,
When this mortality had power
  So to o'ershadow HIM!
That He who gave man's breath might know
  The very depths of human woe.

He proved them all,—the doubt, the strife,
   The faint, perplexing dread,
The mists that hang o'er parting life,
   All gathered round his head;
And the Deliverer knelt to pray,—
Yet passed it not—that cup—away!

It passed not,—though the stormy wave
   Had sunk beneath his tread;
It passed not,—though to him the grave
   Had yielded up its dead.
But there was sent him from on high
A gift of strength for man to die.

And was the sinless thus beset
   With anguish and dismay?
How may *we* meet our conflict yet,
   In the dark, narrow way?
Through Him,—through him that path who trod;
   Save, or we perish, Son of God!

                    MRS. HEMANS.

WOULDST thou inherit life with Christ on high?
     Then count the cost, and know
     That here on earth below
Thou needs must suffer with thy Lord, and die.
We reach that gain, to which all else is loss,
     But through the cross.

Oh think what sorrows Christ himself has known!
  The scorn and anguish sore,
  The bitter death he bore,
Ere he ascended to his heavenly throne;
 And deemest thou thou canst with right complain,
  Whate'er thy pain?

Not e'en the sharpest sorrows we can feel,
  Nor keenest pangs, we dare
  With that great bliss compare
When God his glory shall in us reveal,
That shall endure, when our brief woes are o'er,
  For evermore!

SIMON DACH, 1640.

Ah, Grace! into unlikeliest hearts
  It is thy boast to come,
The glory of thy light to find
  In darkest spots a home.

How will they die, how will they die,
  How bear the cross of grief,
Who have not got the light of faith,
  The courage of belief?

The crowd of cares, the weightiest cross
  Seem trifles less than light, —
Earth looks so little and so low
  When faith shines full and bright.

FABER.

CHAPTER XII.

THE HISTORICAL CHRIST — CHRISTIANITY BASED UPON SUPERNATURAL FACTS — NOT IDEALISM — THE SUPPER A MONUMENT — PHILOSOPHY, THE TRUE AND THE FALSE — POETRY.

"And the Word was made flesh, and dwelt among us." — John 1:14.

WITH a show of wisdom it has been said, "The facts of Christianity are temporary, the ideas eternal." And "an eminent philosopher has judged that Christ himself would be perfectly satisfied if he should find Christianity — that is, sentiments conformed to his views and principles — predominating in the souls of men, whether men valued or neglected his service." . . . . But "it is absolutely impossible in the Christian religion to separate doctrine from the person, to thrust out Christ and yet retain Christianity. . . . . Its essence does not consist of views, principles, and general conclusions."[1] It has an historic basis, an objective reality. Facts enter into its very essence, and constitute it what it is, — a system of regeneration and salvation. The life and death and resurrection of Christ are the foundation of Christianity, with which Christianity stands or falls. That Christ, the Son of God, became incarnate, — the Son of man, dwelling among men, — subject to the laws and conditions of our earthly existence, yet sinless; that in our nature he illustrated the duty and beauty of obedience, the qualities of a perfect manhood, leading a life of benevolence and devotion; that he at length gave himself up to the death of the cross, as an offering for sin; and that on the third day he rose from the tomb, and, after forty days, ascended visibly to his native heaven, — these facts are wrought into the very substance of Christianity, and are inseparable from it, — its "very life and breath and blood." They are not the mere shell, but the meat and marrow; not the outer frame, but the beating heart itself; not the scaffolding and threshold, but the glorious temple. They are not that which conceals, or prepares for, and leads to something better, something more real and enduring; but rather that for

[1] Julius Müller. *Sermons, Bibliotheca Sacra.*

which everything else had been making ready, to be the theatre of which the world was created, and which shall forever be the wonder and inspiration and joy of the holy. Christ is Christianity; not Christ as "a type of humanity, his life and death and resurrection the symbol of the life and death and resurrection of humanity,"[1] and therefore himself to fade away before the rising splendors of that new humanity into which he has passed and in which he is lost,— a mere stepping-stone upon which humanity may mount, and upon which it may trample as having performed its humble service and being no more needed; not such a Christ as subtle skeptics dream of,— but the living, personal Christ, whom Apostles preached as coming to re-create humanity, and be forever its glorious Lord; whose power cannot be limited nor his splendor dimmed; who shall be the eternal bond of heavenly union, and the object of universal and everlasting praise.

This subtle infidelity professes indeed to accept and reverence Christianity, yea, to hold it in its purest form, as an "absolute" religion existing apart from the historic Christ, — as real, as true, as entire, without as with him, nay, as transcend-

---

[1] See Farrar's *Crit. Hist. of Free Thought*.

ing all that is historical and phenomenal, the low region of the senses, of the material, of facts, and therefore more purely spiritual, and so more thoroughly Christian. Beneath the facts of Christianity, regarded as mere external wrappings, these philosophers — falsely so called — assume to reach its "eternal ideas," the final, infinite, absolute Truth itself, in its pure, abstract essence. The incarnation, the life of Christ, all the sacred scenes of the garden and the cross and the tomb, melt away beneath their satanic touch into airy nothing, while to the enraptured vision of the soul abstracted from the material and outward and conditioned, Absolute Truth is revealed as an object of immediate consciousness. Thus, say they, the soul is united to God, and attains the end and perfection of its nature, — absorbed into the great "Over-soul" of the universe, — the pantheistic paradise of philosophical dreamers.

Assailing the historical basis of our faith, this vaunting demon of speculation leaves us at last no Bible, no Christ, no hope; it obliterates "musty parchments," churches and ordinances. For the guilty soul, burdened with sin and panting for pardon, only ideas remain, the atonement is resolved into a mere abstraction, the cross is only a symbol, a help for the weak-minded, but an incumbrance to be shaken off by the strong, and left behind till it recedes at last into a dim, meaningless speck, as the soul, abstracted from the material, soars upward to the Infinite.

An impossible heaven,—for it leaves out the "Lamb that was slain," the only Power that can lift fallen man up to God.

This is perhaps the subtlest phase of hostility to the gospel, having a peculiar charm for a certain class of minds in our day; but well may "the heart speak forth its terror at the idea of losing its most sacred hope, the object of its deepest trust, an historic Saviour."[1] How utterly unsatisfactory is such a theory, with all its high-sounding phrases, to meet the cravings of man's nature and give substantial peace. "Abstract general ideas can have no significance for the religious life."[2] Wandering, like Noah's dove, the soul will find no rest from its perplexities till it can light upon some firmer basis than brilliant ideas. It will still fly on uneasy wing till it finds shelter in the Wounded Heart; and there it abides forever.

[1] Farrar. *Critical History of Free Thought.*
[2] Neander. *Planting and Training of the Christian Church.*

Human nature is renewed in Christ. Christ is "all in all." This is the uniform testimony of Scripture, — of apostles and evangelists and of Christ himself. The Redeemer's earthly life was traced with sacred carefulness, and everywhere proclaimed by inspired teachers, as an indispensable object of faith. Apostles did not preach an abstract system, but what they had "seen and heard," — a personal Christ. "I delivered unto you first of all, that which also I received, how that Christ died for our sins, according to the Scriptures; and that he was buried, and that he rose again the third day, according to the Scriptures; and that he was seen of Cephas, then of the twelve; after that he was seen of above five hundred brethren at once." "That which was from the beginning, which we have heard, which we have seen with our eyes, which we have looked upon, and which our hands have handled, of the Word of life; . . . . that which we have *seen and heard,* declare we unto you."

"The earliest hope of mankind was centred in a *Person,*"[1] and when that Person appeared as Jesus of Nazareth, he was proclaimed as "*the*

---

[1] Westcott. *Introd. to the Study of the Gospels.*

Truth," the perfect and unchangeable fulfilment of that hope.

We cannot doubt that Christ intended the Supper to be a perpetual monument to his personality, and to that personality as the substance of Christianity; and therefore as a continual protest against the speculations of human wisdom. It ever points to Christ, it bids us remember him, and show forth his death, until he come. It rebukes the rash endeavor to put Christianity above Christ, or to hold it apart from Christ, — to view it as in any sort disconnected with his person and his death. It represents Christ as ever the same, — the central object, — still living, and again to come, — the alone hope of our race. It ever bids us, in the touching simplicity and tenderness of its appeals, to believe in the Son of Mary, who was also the Son of God; to believe in his incarnation, his death and resurrection; to seek the remission of our sins and reconciliation to God and the new-creation of our natures through his redeeming blood, and to look for his second advent to judge the world, to glorify his people, and be their life and joy and praise through eternal ages.

Thus the Lord's Supper is one of the monuments of our faith, dear to the Christian heart as the memorial of One who is infinitely precious. Let us then cherish and guard and duly observe this ordinance, for this reason among others, that as an argument for Christianity there is nothing so unanswerable as *Christ himself*. In the Supper, Christ witnesses for his own religion. He recalls the world and the church from its forgetfulness of him, and bids them look and believe and live.[1] In the institution of the Supper, we see him expressing the utmost confidence in the perpetuity and triumph of his religion, and in his own personal enthronement in the memories and hearts of men. He acted as though he expected to be remem-

---

[1] Testimony of an infidel. "In one of those soirées of Baron d' Holback, where the most celebrated infidels of the age were in the habit of assembling, great entertainment was afforded by the witty way in which the pretended absurdities, stupidities, and follies of all kinds which abound in the sacred writers were descanted upon.

"The philosopher Diderot, who had himself taken no part in the conversation, put an abrupt end to it by suddenly saying, 'Gentlemen, I know no men, in France or elsewhere, who can speak or write with more talent or more art. Nevertheless, in spite of all the evil we have spoken of this book [the Bible], I defy you, with all your power, to compose a narrative which shall be as simple but at the same time as sublime and as touching as the recital of the passion and death of Jesus Christ, which shall produce the same effect, and make so strong a sensation, felt so generally by all, and the influence of which shall continue after so many ages.' This unexpected apostrophe astonished all who heard it, and was followed by a long silence." — *Note in Stier's Words of the Lord Jesus*, Vol. 7, p. 435.

bered and loved and adored,—that his "death of agony and shame should never be forgotten while the world lasted." "He took bread and gave it to his disciples, saying, This is my body broken for you; this do in remembrance of me. In like manner he took the cup, saying, This is my blood shed for you; this do in remembrance of me."

"Was ever serenity like this? Can anything more touching, more sublime than this be conceived? Jesus Christ, about to be crucified as a felon and a slave, commanded and provided that the fact should be remembered to the end of time, did so in the full confidence that he should at last triumph. And the fact *has been* remembered. This is the mystery,—if he be not all that he claimed to be,—this is truly more miraculous than anything ever so called, more inexplicable on all natural principles. The fact has been remembered for eighteen hundred years; it is remembered at this day; and it has been, and is remembered, not as a form, a time-honored custom, but minds have been won to Christ, human hearts have been and are inviolably attached to him.

Christ's assurance of triumph is a historical fact; his actual triumph for nearly two thousand years is no less historically certain; the two combined lead to one conclusion only. It is this, — *he* was, as he claimed to be, divine; his religion is divine, the only religion which contains the indubitable proof, and presents to the world a real incarnation of divinity, — God *in* man."[1] And so, if it proves that he is the Son of God, himself divine, and his religion divine, it proves that he is himself the inalienable, inseparable, essential substance of that religion, for this he declared in a variety of forms and in the most unequivocal manner. "Beware [then] lest any man spoil you through philosophy and vain deceit;" and learn to "avoid profane and vain babblings and oppositions of science falsely so called." True philosophy and true science are not hostile to faith, but essentially coincident with revealed religion. They have their important uses when confined to their proper spheres. They may be helpers to our faith. "Not only is philosophy a necessary result of our being and condition, but it is full of benefit, for the more a man knows his own nature, the more will he feel the adaptation of Christianity to it, and be persuaded of its divine origin."[2] But a false philosophy, proud, vaunting, and self-reliant, is full of peril to the mind which yields to its influence. It is defiant,

---

[1] Young. *The Christ of History.* [2] Eadie. *Com. on Colossians.*

rash, blasphemous, — its very spirit proving its falseness, for true philosophy is modest, humble, reverent, as seeking to ascertain facts, and rejoicing in the light which the divine Spirit promises to those that ask it, and ever delighting rather to build up and establish than to destroy, rather to encourage a devout faith than the spirit of speculation. The true philosophy helps to set one's feet on the Rock of ages, the false to lure the deceived mind far out upon a restless sea, where it floats without chart or compass, ever dreaming of some grand discovery, but, unless it retrace its steps in the light of revelation, destined to be swallowed up in the dark abyss of error, or stranded on some far-off and starless shore.

Thanks to the Son of God for the institution of the Supper, which perpetually calls us from our speculative wanderings to his own Person and his own most blessed teachings and his promised Spirit of Truth.

In the light of Incarnate Wisdom and Love we become "wise unto salvation, through faith that is in Christ Jesus." "In the person and work of Christ there is the highest possible manifestation both of the divine power and the divine wisdom.

And those who are "called" not only see but experience this. The doctrine of Christ crucified produces effects on them which nothing short of divine power can accomplish. And it reveals and imparts to them the true wisdom. It makes them divinely wise; it makes them holy; it makes them righteous; it makes them blessed. It does infinitely more than human wisdom could ever conceive, much less accomplish. It has already changed the state of the intelligent universe, and is to be the central point of influence throughout eternity. This is the doctrine which the wise of this world wish to see ignored or obscured in behalf of their speculations. Just as the heathen exchange the true God for birds and beasts and creeping things, and think themselves profound."[1] To thee, then, O Christ, will we forever cling.

JESUS, these eyes have never seen
That radiant form of thine!
The vail of sense hangs dark between
Thy blessed face and mine.

[1] Dr. Hodge. *Com. on 1 Cor.*

I see thee not, I hear thee not,
  Yet art thou oft with me;
And earth hath ne'er so dear a spot
  As where I meet with thee.

Like some bright dream that comes unsought,
  When slumbers o'er me roll,
Thine image ever fills my thought,
  And charms my ravished soul.

Yet though I have not seen, and still
  Must rest in faith alone;
I love thee, dearest Lord, and will,
  Unseen, but not unknown.

When death these mortal eyes shall seal,
  And still this throbbing heart,
The rending vail shall thee reveal,
  All glorious as thou art!

PALMER.

HERE, O my Lord, I see thee face to face,
  Here would I touch and handle things unseen;
Here grasp with firmer hand th' eternal grace,
  And all my weariness upon thee lean.

Here would I feed upon the Bread of God,
  Here drink with thee the royal wine of heaven;
Here would I lay aside each earthly load,
  Here taste afresh the calm of sin forgiven.

Mine is the sin, but thine the righteousness;
  Mine is the guilt, but thine the cleansing blood.
This is my robe, my refuge and my peace, —
  Thy blood, thy righteousness, O Lord my God!

Too soon we rise; the symbols disappear;
  The feast, but not the love, is passed and gone;
The bread and wine remove, but thou art here, —
  Nearer than ever, — still my shield and sun.

Feast after feast thus comes and passes by;
  Yet, passing, points to the great feast above,
Giving sweet foretastes of the festal joy,
  The Lamb's great bridal feast of bliss and love.

H. BONAR.

The golden palace of my God
  Towering above the clouds I see;
Beyond the cherubs' bright abode,
  Higher than angels' thoughts can be.
How can I in those courts appear
  Without a wedding-garment on?
Conduct me, thou Life-giver, there,
  Conduct me to thy glorious throne!
And clothe me with thy robes of light,
And lead me through sin's darksome night,
  My Saviour and my God.

From the Russian.

CHAPTER XIII.

A PERSONAL CHRIST — EXPERIENCE OF PRESIDENT EDWARDS — STODDARD — DR. ARNOLD — ARTHUR HALLAM — THE RELATION OF THE SUPPER TO CHRIST'S PERSONALITY — POETRY.

"*Come unto me, ... and I will give you Rest.*" — *Matt 11 : 28.*

UPON this subject — a personal Christ — we may profitably dwell a little longer. It has most important practical bearings.

The God of the philosophers of this world is not the God of the Bible. He is a cold, impassive Being, more an abstraction than a living Reality, more a negation of human attributes than a positive existence, dwelling far apart from our earthly sphere, without sympathy, with scarce any points of loving, confidential connection between him and his creatures, with no affections answering to theirs, — a being to be regarded with awe and dread, as infinite Power.

But in the Bible, — that precious revelation of our Heavenly Father, — God is represented to us in a very different way. Yet it is a way accordant with a true philosophy, which takes cognizance of the real wants and cravings of our nature, — wants and cravings of God's own awakening, and therefore having, of necessity, something answering to them and satisfying them, in God's own nature. "We are taught that there is One, ... even the only-begotten Son of God, who dwelt upon earth for the very purpose of breathing a new life of faith into us, of setting a living object of faith before us; so that, in every need and peril, whithersoever the chances of the world may waft us, we shall see God, not afar off in the heavens, in the clouds of speculation or the dim twilight of tradition, but close by our side, as our Example, our Guide, our Friend, our Brother, our Saviour, and Redeemer."[1]

"Once," wrote President Edwards, " as I rode out into the woods, having alighted from my horse in a retired place, as my manner commonly has been, to walk for divine contemplation and prayer, I had a view, that for me was extraordinary, of the glory of the Son of God, as Mediator between

---

[1] Rev. J. C. Hare. *Mission of the Comforter.*

God and man, and his wonderful, great, full, pure, and precious grace and love, and meek and gentle condescension. This grace that appeared so calm and sweet appeared also great above the heavens. The person of Christ appeared ineffably excellent, with an excellency great enough to swallow up all thought and conception." At another time he says, "It appeared sweet, beyond all expression, to follow Christ, and to be taught and enlightened and instructed by him, to learn of him and live to him."

Of that devoted missionary to the Nestorians, David Tappan Stoddard, a friend wrote: "To an unusual degree he attained to habits of spirituality, and close intimacy with the Saviour. He walked with him as with an elder brother. With all possible fulness and confidence he breathed his heart's sorrows into his ear; and this was the secret of that serenity and spiritual hilarity which diffused itself through his life. In him, religion robed herself in her most winning garb. . . . . If any pilgrim ever turned this valley of Baca (*weeping*) into a well, and through this vale of tears carried a heart full of melody, he was that one. . . . He kept the words of Jesus, and Jesus came and made his abode with him, and manifested himself unto him."[1]

The religious life of Dr. Arnold presents no more interesting feature than "the peculiar feeling of love and adoration which he entertained toward our Lord Jesus Christ," regarding "not only his work of redemption, but *Himself*, as a living Friend and Master." Believing most fully in his supreme deity, and yet that he was "still the self-same Jesus in all human affections and divine excellences," there was, says his biographer, "a vividness and tenderness in his conception of him on which, if one may so say, all his feelings of human friendship and affection seemed to fasten, as on their natural object."[2]

The great Jonathan Edwards and the humble freedwoman, Phebe Ann Jacobs, both of blessed memory, alike spoke of "*holding Christ by the hand.*" Said the latter, "My little home has become *a palace;* while sweeping my room to-day, I thought I must sweep softly, for he was here, my Lord and King."

This is the glory of Christianity, that it reveals in the eternal God what the lofty and the lowly, the profound scholar and the illiterate slave, alike

---

[1] *Memoir of Stoddard.*   [2] *Life and Correspondence.*

need to find, — the nearest and dearest friend, in the person of Jesus Christ, the Son of God and the Son of man. In Christ, we feel that the heart of God beats in sympathy with us. God is our Father.

Christianity calls us not merely to accept a system of doctrines from a great teacher, which we are to make the basis of moral improvement, but above all and as comprehending all the rest, to love, trust in, adore, and imitate that Being who lived and died for us.

> "Talk they of morals? O thou bleeding Love,
> The grand morality is love of thee."

It is to him we are to be united in living fellowship, — himself the life of our souls and the object of our faith. It is the sweet consciousness of his living presence that is to give delight to duty, dignity to the humblest service, power to overcome temptation; that is to shed a heavenly radiance over the dark hours of suffering, and even light up the vale of death,[1] — Christ the "hope of glory."

---

[1] "Provision is made in the Scriptures for meeting the peculiar sentiment which the Christian's conjoined faith in the unseen world, and ignorance of its conditions, engenders. And, as matter of fact, the

"One with Christ," "growing up into Christ," "to be with Christ,"—this sums up all the possibilities of bliss and spiritual attainment. "I looked," said one, "to the world for enjoyment; it failed me. I looked to a prosperous business for wealth, balanced loss and profit, and I had

dying expressions of multitudes of the faithful, in every age, have exemplified the fitness of this provision to the occasion. . . . . The palpitating heart must appropriate the *personal affection* of the Redeemer to his people. THIS APPROPRIATION is the secret of dying. The human mind, when once thoroughly occupied by a benign affection, specially fixed upon its object, can meet any danger, can brave any dismay. History abounds with illustrations of this fact; it is a capital law of our nature. Men, nay women, thus animated, have forgotten all fear, and carried themselves through fields of death as calmly as if they had none but an etherial frame. If we analyze our emotions on any occasions of this sort, we shall find that if at any time a steady courage has borne us with force and animation and cheerfulness through hours of imminent peril, it has been when we have had to act on behalf of those most dear to us; or when the welfare of such has depended altogether upon our conduct. Even the martial courage of the field, if it be more than animal bravery, is constituted on the same principle, and would be nothing if stripped of its affections."—*Isaac Taylor, Saturday Evening.*

"One does not perhaps fear so much the pains of death—what is often incorrectly termed the agonies of dissolution—as he does the launching out on an unknown sea, alone; plunging into darkness, entering into a boundless space, where there is nothing tangible, local, or visible; where the soul leaves behind all the warm sympathies of life, all which can communicate with other beings. However fortified by faith, it seems to be a dread experiment. We cling instinctively to some sure support, some familiar surrounding objects.

"But is it not a thought full of comfort, that, to the believer, his Renothing. I looked to my sons for comfort and support; they died. I looked to JESUS, and found comfort, support, enjoyment, riches, redemption, *everything*. 'Looking to Jesus,' I expect to reach heaven for my last home, where I shall see him in his glory." Said J— R—,[1] of N——, after the death of his wife and children, "I am all alone, and my property is run down so that I am very poor; but it all makes no odds. Christ doesn't die, Christ isn't poor, Christ never leaves me, Christ is always with me; I know him and have seen him, and anybody who has ever seen him once will never want anything else, if he can only have him."

"To see Christ," said the late Dr. Raffles, as he lay dying, — "to see Christ, that is heaven!"

deemer stands at the very threshold of death, the other side of that thin curtain which hides mortality from life; stands there, not as an abstract form, or an impalpable vision, but *as a dear friend*, with his heart overflowing with human sympathies! It is like meeting on a foreign shore our best earthly friend, perfectly familiar with the language and all the objects there; a guide most intelligent, most faithful, who will anticipate every desire, and in whose society we find the sweetest contentment and the largest accessions of knowledge and delight." — *Rev. B. B. Edwards. Extract from a Sermon. From Memoirs, by Rev. Prof. Park.*

[1] This man, from being a low, profane, intemperate vagrant, was suddenly transformed by the grace of God (in the year 1824) into an humble, earnest, benevolent, devout, and happy Christian.

"What would the gathering of a court be," said his friend and former companion in labors, Angell James, "without the *king?*" "Oh," said another of kindred spirit, "for the shadows to flee away, that I might *look,* and be filled with his overcoming love!"[1] Said Samuel Budgett, the Christian merchant, on the eve of his departure, "I this day hang like a little child in a brook catching hold of a branch that is thrown out to save it; only there is this one difference in my case, I hang on the Branch of Jesse's stem. Christ will keep me, and I am safe. . . . . I like to hear of the beauties of heaven; but I do not dwell upon them,— no, what I rejoice in is this, that *Christ will be there.*"[2]

Just after the battle of Williamsburg, a chaplain of the Christian Commission was hastily summoned to the side of a dying soldier. He found him pale and blood-stained from a terrible wound above the temple. The first request was that the chaplain would cut from his forehead a lock for his mother. "Now," said he, "I want you to kneel down and return thanks to God for such a mother. And thank God that by his grace I am a Christian. Oh, what would I do now if I wasn't a Christian!

[1] *The Presbyterian.* [2] *Life of Samuel Budgett.*

I know that my Redeemer liveth. I feel that his finished work has saved me. And thank God for giving me dying grace. He has made my dying bed

'Feel soft as downy pillows are.'

Thank him for the promised home in glory. I'll soon be there, — there, where there is no war, no sorrow, nor desolation, nor death; where *I'll see Jesus, and be forever with the Lord.*"

It has been nobly remarked: " There exists in the doctrine of the cross a peculiar and inexhaustible treasure for the affectionate feelings. The idea of the Θεανθρωπος [God-man], the God whose goings forth have been from everlasting, yet visible to men for their redemption as an earthly temporal creature, living, acting, and suffering among themselves; then, — which is yet more important, — transferring to the unseen place of his spiritual agency the same humanity he wore on earth, so that the lapse of generations can in no way effect the conception of his identity; this is the most powerful thought that ever addressed itself to a human imagination. . . . . Here was solved at once the great problem which so long had distressed the teachers of mankind, how to make *virtue the object of passion,* and to secure at once the warmest enthusiasm in the heart with the clearest perception of right and wrong in the understanding. The character of the blessed Founder of our faith became an abstract of morality to determine the judgment, *while at the same time it remained personal and liable to love.*" [1]

In this view we see how profoundly appropriate was the thrice repeated question to the son of Jonas, "Lovest thou *me?*" It was all-comprehensive. It satisfied all the conditions of holiness. It covered the entire ground of duty and happiness. It invested all that is true and good and excellent with the attraction of a personal love. It called, not for the admiration of abstract principles and precepts, an abstract Christianity, but for the love of a *Person*, who embodied in himself all possible excellences, and who through inconceivable sufferings, had performed for us a work, and secured for us benefits, of transcendent worth.

To make his personality more emphatic and impressive was perhaps one design of his residence on earth for so many years. For aught we know, he might have accomplished his redemptive work by a very brief sojourn among men. In a week or a day, he might have consummated his incarnation

[1] Arthur Hallam, quoted in *Spare Hours.*

by bearing our sins on the cross, and then have passed at once to his native heaven. But how indistinct the impression of his person! It would have seemed more like a strange phantasm, an "incorporeal image," as the Docetae dreamed, than like a reality. But the extension of his earthly life to thirty years has imparted a wonderful distinctness and vividness to our conception of the historical Christ. He lives and moves before us in the beauty and glory of his divine humanity.

In this view we see the significance and value of the ordinance of the Supper. As we hear the voice of Jesus, "This is my body," "Remember me," a living Person rises to view, and there passes before us all his marvellous life of love. We hear his advent announced; we see him, "that holy thing," the babe in the manger; we see him in his strange, beautiful childhood; we follow him as he "went about doing good," discoursing wisdom, healing diseases, comforting the afflicted, preaching the gospel, and, especially, as the bread is broken and the wine poured out, in his mysterious agonies, — bearing his cross, fainting beneath its burden, and hanging upon it! we see the wounds, the blood; we hear the death-cry; and we know that "God was manifest in the flesh." Here is a personal Christ; here he meets his disciples; here he comes near to them; here he bids them welcome; here he shows them his hands and his feet and his side; here he invites the weary and penitent to come and receive of the riches of his grace. Surely, from this scene we may go away, saying, We have seen the Lord. With a deeper feeling of its truth may we say, Here is a Brother, a Friend, with whom, as our Guide and Helper, we may walk through the world up to our eternal home.

But the symbols of Christ's incarnation are very simple, only suggestive of the physical and visible, so that our thoughts may soon soar on the wings of faith to behold him in his more exalted and glorious form. "The Word," says Alford, "became one flesh with us, that we might become one spirit in him," which would have been hindered by a perpetual beholding of his humanity. Therefore was he removed from the immediate range of mere earthly vision, that we might more readily rise to the conception of that wondrous Person who, in his divine majesty, sits at the right hand of the Father. He is a King; but even in his glory he is still our Brother. "He soared to heaven with a spirit as lowly as the grave he left; thus beats there at the right hand of the Majesty on high, a human heart, — the heart of an enthroned King, — more softly subdued to mercy, more meekly patient, than ever sorrowed among the loneliest solitudes of earthly affliction."[1]

"My hand in Christ's!" He leadeth where he lists,
    Through flowery fields, or 'neath a starry sky;
My faith is strong; *he'll* bring me safely through
    The ills of life, till I am called to die.

"My hand in Christ's!" I care not how death comes,
    Whether by pestilence or in the fight;
I shall be safe beneath his gentle care,
    Should the sun smite by day or the moon by night.

"My hand in Christ's!" who bore up Calvary's height
    The cross, and gave his precious life up there
To save a wretch like me! Can I e'er doubt,
    Or give myself a victim to despair?

No; let me cling the closer to his side,
    And with a child's devotion hold him fast;
"My hand in his!" I'll safely pass along;
    Though storms may howl, my home I'll gain at last.

[1] William Archer Butler. *Sermons.*

"My hand in Christ's!" e'en down to death's cold flood,
  He'll bear me conqueror through the dying strife;
And safe with those who've only gone before,
  I shall have entered on that higher life.

  Holy Saviour, friend unseen,
  Since on thy arm thou bidst me lean,
  Help me throughout life's varying scene,
    By faith to cling to thee!

  Blest with this fellowship divine,
  Take what thou wilt, I'll ne'er repine;
  E'en as the branches to the vine,
    My soul would cling to thee!

  Far from her home, fatigued, opprest,
  Here she has found her place of rest;
  An exile still, yet not unblest,
    While she can cling to thee!

  Oft, when I seem to tread alone
  Some barren waste with thorns o'ergrown,
  Thy voice of love, in tenderest tone,
    Whispers, "Still cling to me!"

  Though faith and hope may oft be tried,
  I ask not, need not, aught beside;
  How safe, how calm, how satisfied,
    The soul that clings to thee!

Blest is my lot, whate'er befall;
What can disturb me, what appall,
Whilst as my rock, my strength, my all,
    Saviour, I cling to thee?

Hymns of the Ages.

"LORD, hadst thou been here
My brother had not died!" The Saviour groaned
In spirit, and stooped tenderly and raised
The mourner from the ground, and in a voice
Broke in its utterance like her own, he said,
"Where have ye laid him?" Then the Jews who came,
Following Mary, answered, through their tears,
"Lord, come and see!" But, lo! the mighty heart
That in Gethsemane sweat drops of blood,
Taking for us the cup that might not pass, —
The heart whose breaking cord upon the cross
Made the earth tremble and the sun afraid
To look upon his agony, — the heart
Of a lost world's Redeemer, — overflowed,
Touched by a mourner's sorrow! JESUS WEPT!

WILLIS.

OFT, as the daylight hours were gone,
    When friends forsook and foes beset,
The Saviour of the world, alone,
    Retired to pray on Olivet.

And still by faith I climb its steep,
  A respite from earth's cares to find,
To hush distracting thoughts asleep,
  Amid the sabbath of the mind.

The saint in glory owns and sees
  A brother in the man of prayer;
The little infant on its knees
  Is kinsman to each seraph there!

CHAPTER XIV.

THE SOCIAL ASPECT OF THE SUPPER — BROTHERLY LOVE — IM-
PROPER INFERENCE — DR. JUDSON — POETRY.

"The household of faith." — Gal. 6 : 10.

COMMUNION — the communion of the saints — is expressed by the Lord's Supper. Here a *family* is gathered around a common table, for mutual greetings, and the supply of similar wants by a joint participation of the same food. Here Jesus meets his assembled disciples. The table is spread for the church, and not for the members in their individual capacity. "We are all partakers of that one loaf."

Such was the character of the ordinance as instituted by the Saviour, and as observed in apostolic times. The disciples "came together to break bread."

Baptism must, of necessity, be an eminently individual act, even when several believers are baptized at once, for it indicates the entrance upon the new life in Christ. This takes place from the Spirit breathing as he will upon the dead in sin, quickening to life now one and then another; and such new-born child is expected for himself to give outward expression to the great fact of his new creation in Christ Jesus, by a symbolic burial and rising with Christ.[1]

But when individual births have multiplied, and there results a Christian family organized under the law of its Head, then may the members of that household meet together to symbolize, by a special outward act, the *continuance and sustenance* of that divine life in Christ which they share alike, and whose commencement was signified by baptism. Hence it is that the Supper properly follows baptism, as the support of life succeeds to the beginning of life.[2]

How naturally, then, are Christians drawn together, and especially at the Lord's Table. They

---

[1] Rom. vi. 4.

[2] "As regeneration, the commencing-point in the Christian life, is represented by baptism, so is this, the sequel of regeneration, the continued regeneration, as it were, of man, the continued incorporation of mankind into the body of Christ, represented by the Supper." — *Neander, Planting and Training of the Church.*

are one in Christ, alike dependent on his grace, members of his mystical body, growing up into him their living Head by faith in that great Sacrifice which is symbolized by the broken bread and poured-out wine. And how thankful should they be that Christ's own wisdom and love have provided for the wants of their spiritual and social natures, in the Supper.

Social worship, at stated seasons, is a divine appointment and a religious necessity. They who are one in Christ cannot remain apart. They must speak often one to another.

The Sabbath bell summons the Christian family together to adore their common Father and Redeemer. In other religious gatherings do they show their brotherly oneness in Christ. In Christian homes, there is an altar around which pious hearts love to meet and lay their common offerings, and renew and cement more closely their endeared mutual fellowship.

Christ is the common bond of all these unions, — the object of common trust and love.

But where is this heaven-born longing for fellowship with one another and with Christ, so fitly expressed and so fully met as at the Lord's Table?

Here preëminently do Christians come together as a family, at the social board. "A table is an emblem of home. Influences centre round our tables, not exceeded in their power and interest elsewhere. Happy hours pass by, bonds of love are formed, are nurtured; . . . . friendships are cemented, and alienations are healed there. . . . . The table is the central point of all domestic comforts and blessings. . . . When Christianity chooses a table as a symbol of her choicest gifts, we see how eminently social and benevolent its nature is, — common fellowship, giving, the rites of hospitality, invigoration and cheer, and every plausible idea which comes at the thought of a welcome table, are implied in it."[1]

At the Lord's Supper, Christians symbolize more perfectly their oneness in Christ and their future heavenly fellowship than at any other religious gatherings; for here, if the table is duly guarded, none are found but the Heavenly Father's children, disciples of Christ, brethren in the Lord, joint-heirs with Jesus Christ. Here they sit, apart and separate from the world, a Christian family, a flock gathered out from the wilderness, com-

---

[1] Dr. Adams. *The Communion Sabbath.*

memorating the love of the Good Shepherd, who laid down his life for his sheep. Here they partake of the Bread of Life, the common nutriment of their spiritual nature; here they see that flowing blood which is the cementing bond; and thus do they show their identification with Christ, as " bone of his bone, flesh of his flesh," and thus' their own oneness in him, " in whom all the building, fitly framed together, groweth into an holy temple in the Lord." " The cup of blessing which we bless, is it not the *communion* of the blood of Christ? The bread which we break, is it not the *communion* of the body of Christ? For we being many are one bread and one body; for *we are all partakers of that one bread.*"[1]

"As many grains of wheat, ground and kneaded and compacted, form the unity of a single loaf of bread, thus many believers, joined to Christ, and joined to each other, form one corporate structure of Christian community. The two leading thoughts are, therefore, that believers have communion or participation or fellowship with Christ; and that in this they have fellowship with one another. This is set forth by the one loaf and the one cup."[1]

---

[1] 1 Cor. x. 16. [2] Dr. J. W. Alexander. *Sacramental Discourses.*

How deeply affecting is the spectacle, — such a company, at such a table! How must it attract the admiring gaze of angels! As they speed their way over the earth, glad messengers of God's will, and witness the terrible workings of sin, — the blind worldliness that rushes on in unbelief and impenitence, regardless of God's authority and mercy, — the hatreds that drive men asunder, or together only for mutual destruction, fearfully typical of hell, — we may readily imagine them pausing in their course, and reverently folding their wings, as they come upon such a scene, seemingly so foreign to earth, perhaps in some retired and humble sanctuary or some obscure upper-room, — a happy family in Christ, redeemed by precious blood, regenerate by the quickening Spirit, separated from the jars and strifes of the world, — a scene so peaceful, so still, so radiant with love, so suggestive of a present Christ, as to be no unfit emblem of heavenly communion and peace.

How powerfully, then, does this ordinance persuade to *brotherly love!* Here is indicated a union which shall outlast all the tenderest and strongest of earthly fellowships. Here *they* sit together who are expecting to meet at the marriage supper of the Lamb.

Shall the members of Christ's body — "members one of another" — be at variance with each other and with their Head? That were a spectacle which might well make angels weep, and which must grieve the holy and loving Spirit. Shall that family which hopes to meet unbroken on the other side the river fall out by the way-side as it journeys thither?

> "Oh, how shall envious brethren own
> A Brother on the eternal throne,
> Their Father's joy, their hope alone?"

O brethren among whom the enemy has been sowing discord, here see that you are one, — one in Christ, — and here bury your strifes and envies, here rise above the petty differences of opinion and feeling that have divided those whom death cannot part, whose fellowship shall be eternal. May the blood of atonement melt all hearts into one, and thus make the communion season an antepast of heaven.

But while this ordinance, as "the Lord's *Supper*," is for the *church*, and is of a *social* character, yet it is for the church as composed of *individuals*, holding each a *personal relation to Christ* which infinitely surpasses their fellowship with each other.

They are to remember Christ, and renew their personal covenant with him and their personal appropriation of his grace. To this distinguishing feature of the ordinance its social aspect is altogether subordinate. The admiring gaze of each and all is to be directed to Christ the common Saviour, and it is this singleness of eye which indicates the essential unity of the church. They are one, they are brethren, they are a family, because Christ is the one all-absorbing object of attraction and trust. The fellowship is broken or marred when their thoughts are diverted from him who said, " Do this in remembrance of *me*."

Most unscriptural, then, is absence from the Lord's Table because of some alleged misdemeanor of a fellow-disciple, lest partaking of the elements with the offender should seem to sanction his sin. Can his delinquencies justify my neglect to remember Christ in the ordinance of the Supper?

And shall the commemoration of the death of Christ be confounded with church discipline? Shall one member be judge over the whole body, or be responsible for its discipline?

And shall the very observance of the sacrament be subject to the caprice or judgment of individuals? for if one may rightfully withdraw, then may another, then may all; and what will become of this precious memorial of Christ? Shall it wait the convenience or feelings of individual Christians?

And can we suppose that wholesome discipline would be promoted by a negligent or irregular observance of the Lord's Supper? Surely it must always be well to obey Christ, to remember him and show his death.

O Saviour, may this be to me a memorial hour! May I remember thee, and for thy sake sit meekly and lovingly with my fellow-disciples. And if any seem to have wandered from thee, and to eat and drink unworthily, help me here to pray for them and commend them to thy mercy, deeply sensible, at the same time, of my own frailty and unworthiness and need of mercy. Remember *me*, O Saviour! a poor helpless sinner, and enable me to set such an example before others that their inconsistencies may not be laid at my door. Here breathe thy Spirit of love and truth into my heart, that I may be prepared to deal tenderly and faithfully with wanderers from the cross.

"Crucified Love, thou hast gathered the scattered ones together, and when they meet at the foot of thy cross, they recognize and love one another truly. Oh, there is no other bond of love so firm as that which is formed beneath the cross. There men learn to know sin, and also to forgive sin; and how should they not also learn truly to love? Beneath the sceptre of the crucified King are the scattered sheep first united, and learn to love one another with a new love, and to bear one another's burdens.

"Crucified love, teach me also to love all those whom I meet at the foot of thy cross. I will give them the hand of fellowship, as unto brethren who are travelling with me along the one safe path towards the fatherland; I will forgive them as thou hast forgiven me, and I will love them with thy love."[1]

An interesting passage in the closing scenes of the life of Dr. Judson happily illustrates this subject: "Like all persons of his ardent temperament, he was subject to strong attachments and aversions, which he sometimes had difficulty in bringing under the controlling influence of divine grace. He remarked that he had always felt more or less of an affectionate interest in his brethren, as brethren, and some of them he had loved very dearly for their personal qualities; but he

---

[1] Tholuck. *Hours of Devotion.*

was now aware that he had never placed his standard of love high enough. He spoke of them as children of God, redeemed by the Saviour's blood, watched over and guarded by his love, dear to his heart, honored by him in the election, and to be honored hereafter before the assembled universe; and he said it was not sufficient to be kind and obliging to such, to abstain from evil speaking, and make a general mention of them in our prayers; but our attachment to them should be of the most ardent and exalted character: it would be so in heaven, and we lost immeasurably by not beginning now. 'As I have loved you, so ought ye also to love one another,' was a precept continually in his mind; and he would often murmur, as though unconsciously, 'As I have loved you,'— 'as I have loved you;' then burst out with the exclamation, 'Oh, the love of Christ! the love of Christ!'"

The Lord's Supper is a sacrament, as a memorial of Christ. But, in a secondary sense, in a Christian household, and to the Christian everywhere, every meal should be a sacrament. For is not our ordinary food said " to be sanctified by the Word of God and prayer,"[1] as set apart by such

---

[1] See Hodge on 1 Cor. x. 16.

religious service to the end for which it was appointed?[1] Is it not a memorial of Christ, for does not our daily food come to us through him? Did he not teach us to pray for it? Is it not designed to remind us of God's mercy in Christ, and therefore to be eaten " with gladness and singleness of heart "? Is it not to strengthen the Christian for his Master's service? And especially when the Christian invites to his board a member of Christ's flock, particularly one of Christ's poor, should not the meal be to him a memorial of Christ? Should he not see the Master in the disciple, and feel that he honors Christ in his kindness to one who bears his image and for whom Christ died?

There is a little lonely fold,
   Whose flock one Shepherd keeps
Through summer's heat and winter's cold,
   With eye that never sleeps.

By evil beast, or burning sky,
   Or damp of midnight air,
Not one in all that flock shall die
   Beneath that Shepherd's care.

[1] 1 Tim. iv. 5.

For if, unheeding or beguiled,
  In danger's path they roam,
His pity follows through the wild,
  And guides them safely home.

O gentle Shepherd, still behold
  Thy helpless charge in me;
And take a wanderer to thy fold,
  That, trembling, turns to thee.

Jesus, help conquer!
  My spirit is sinking,,
Deep waters of sorrow go over my head;
  Weeping and trembling
    And fearing and shrinking
I watch for the day, and night cometh instead.
  Bitter the cup
    I am hourly drinking;
How thorny the path that hourly I tread!

  Jesus, help conquer!
    For, fainting and weary,
Scarcely my hands can their weapons sustain;
  The way seems so desolate,
    Painful and dreary, —
How shall I ever to heaven attain?
  Jesus, great Captain,
    If thou be not near me,
How shall I ever the victory gain?

Jesus, help conquer!
 Earth holds out her lure,
And mortal affections yearn after the prize;
 Scarcely my heart
  Can the struggle endure;
'Scarce can I lift up my tear-blinded eyes.
 Jesus, Redeemer,
  Thy promise is sure,—
Speak to my spirit, and bid me arise.

Jesus, help conquer!
 There is not an hour
Of sorrow or joy but is ordered by thee;
 Thou dost cut down,
  Who hast planted the flower;
Tempest or calm at thy bidding shall be.
 Look on my sorrow,
  And give me the power
Humbly to wait till thou comfortest me.

Jesus, help conquer!
 Lord, turn not away!
See with what power the billows increase!
 Give me thy love
  For my comfort and stay;
Then shall my trembling and murmuring cease;
 Then shall my spirit
  Grow strong for the fray;
Then shall my weary heart rest in thy peace.

Jesus, help conquer!
I cry unto thee!
Hardly my heart its petitions can frame;
All is so dark
And so painful to me;
All I can utter, sometimes, is thy name.
Jesus, help conquer!
My portion now be;
Though all else should change, be thou ever the same.

Communion of my Saviour's blood,—
In him to have my lot and part;
To prove the virtue of that flood
Which burst on Calvary from his heart;

To feed by faith on Christ, my Bread,—
His body broken on the tree;
To live in him, my living Head,
Who died and rose again for me;—

This be my joy and comfort here,
This pledge of future glory mine:
Jesus! in spirit now appear,
And break the bread, and pour the wine.

From thy dear hand may I receive
The tokens of thy dying love;
And while I feast on earth, believe
That I shall feast with thee above.

Ah! there, though in the lowest place,
  Thee at thy table could I meet,
And see thee, know thee, face to face;—
  For such a moment death were sweet.

What then will their fruition be,
  Who meet in heaven with blest accord?
A moment? No; eternity!
  They are forever with the Lord.
Haddon Collection.

Jesus, Shepherd of the sheep!
Thou thy flock in safety keep.
Living Bread! thy life supply;
Strengthen us, or else we die;
  Fill us with celestial grace.
Thou who feedest us below,
Source of all we have or know!
Grant that with thy saints above,
Sitting at the feast of love,
  We may see thee face to face.
Missal.

CHAPTER XV.

THE RELATION OF THE SUPPER TO THE IMPENITENT — A SILENT SERMON — SILENT OBSERVANCE — MRS. BETHUNE.

"Behold the Lamb of God, who taketh away the sin of the world!"
John 1:29.

M'CHEYNE, that honored minister of the Free Church of Scotland, whose heart and whose sermons were so full of Christ, says, in one of his discourses, of the Lord's Supper, "It is a *sweet, silent sermon.* Many a sermon contains not Christ from beginning to end. Many show him doubtfully and imperfectly. But here is *nothing else but Christ and him crucified.* Most rich and speaking ordinance! Pray that the very sight of that broken bread may break your hearts and make them flow to the Lamb of God.

"Pray for *conversions* from the sight of the broken bread and poured-out wine. . . . When the Roman centurion that watched beside the cross of Jesus saw him die, and the rocks rend, he cried out, Truly this was the Son of God! Look at this broken bread, and you will see the same thing; and may your heart be made to cry after the Lord Jesus!

"When the dying thief looked on the pale face of Immanuel, and saw the divine majesty that beamed from his dying eye, he cried, Lord, remember me. This broken bread reveals the same thing; may the same grace be given you, and may you breathe the cry, Lord, remember me."[1]

The Saviour teaches us, in this ordinance, not only to remember him, but *to show*[2] *his death*. It is not only commemorative, but declarative. It brings Christ before us as dying for our sins, and declares that there is salvation in none other name. Can it then have been intended alone for the benefit of the church, and not also to bear its message to the unregenerate?

In the sermon which usually precedes the Sup-

---

[1] *M'Cheyne's Works*, Vol. I.

[2] The original word (καταγγέλλετε), rendered, in our common version, "show," signifies to *announce, proclaim, preach*. See Rom. i. 8; Acts iv. 2, xiii. 38.

The Lord's Supper is, "in its very nature, a proclamation of the fact" of Christ's death.

per, the minister lifts up the Son of man, and beseeches his hearers, for Christ's sake, to be reconciled to God. In the Supper, Christ is lifted up in a symbolic crucifixion; "the most important truths of Christianity, which we commonly only hear or read, are visibly set before us, made cognizable to the senses, and exhibited in such a way as powerfully to move the feelings, and make an indelible impression on the memory."[1] It is indeed a "silent sermon," and why should not the audience be as large as possible?

While it would be a profanation of the holy ordinance, and a condemnation to themselves, for the impenitent to partake, because especially it would be the expression of a faith and a love which they do not possess, and a "showing" the death of One in whom they have not trusted for salvation, whom they have in fact rejected, yet for them to "look upon" Him whom they have "pierced," and to listen to his voice of mercy pleading with them in the mute eloquence of an agony unto death, to turn and live, is surely what every Christian heart should desire them to do. Come, stand before the cross, may be the invitation of the church; behold the Saviour suffer and die! Look,

---

[1] Knapp, *Christian Theology*.

and measure, if you can, the love that bowed such a head in death. And measure, if you can, the exceeding sinfulness of sin, which rendered necessary for its atonement and removal so vast a sacrifice. The Son of God in tears and blood! Before your eyes Jesus Christ is evidently set forth among you crucified. See his arms stretched wide, as if to welcome every returning penitent; and those eyes, now closed in death, pleading with you to forsake your sins; and trust your soul into his hands, as a now living Saviour.

This is the language of the ordinance; and why should the congregation be dismissed, and the church alone listen to the discourse? Has it not a solemn, tender word for all? Does it not say, "Whosoever will, let him come"? And who can tell how many, hearing the story of the cross thus told by a united church, in the silent breaking of bread, may be led to Christ, and then, as obedient disciples, coming to the Table, increase the number that publish the "glad tidings"? We have in mind a church not a few of whose members trace their religious awakening to the impression of such a scene witnessed some Sabbath afternoon, in response to the general invitation of the pastor, or the kind solicitation of a Christian friend. Seated apart, they were led to think of that great separation, at the judgment-day, between the friends and foes of Christ, and to ask themselves whether they needed not a personal interest in that atoning blood which was symbolized by the poured-out wine.

And would not Christian parents, seeing their unconverted children sitting thus outside the fold, without hope and without God, be likely to have their anxiety for their salvation deepened? Here a visible line is drawn, here is a separation. Shall it be eternal? Shall they be on the right hand and their children on the left? Will not the cry be begotten in their hearts, O good Shepherd, who didst lay down thy life for the sheep, gather these also into thy fold? Send thy quickening Spirit to convince them of sin and draw them to thy wounded side. And might it not be hoped that the Church, as a body, would feel a more tender concern for those that "are without"? that a deeper sense of responsibility might be rolled upon their consciences? But whatever our conjectures or our belief as to the influence of such a public observance of the Supper, do not the very words of Christ, as to *showing his death*, teach us that this is according to his will? And that is enough. Let not the light of this ordinance be hidden in a corner.

In this view, it is evident that the preliminary services should be short, lest a feeling of weariness should prevent those from remaining to witness the Supper whom the "love of Christ" does not "constrain." In some churches the sermon is omitted, and a few pertinent remarks introduce the solemn and interesting scene.

And to increase its impressiveness, both to the church and the congregation, let it *speak for itself*. It is itself a sermon. It preaches and pleads. Human words, if beyond a few earnest utterances to guide the thoughts of the communicants, seem to be an intrusion upon the sacred eloquence of the scene itself. It is Christ that speaks. Let him be heard. Leave the soul to the remembrance of Christ, to communion with Christ. Here he meets his disciples, — for we believe in the "real presence" of Christ at the eucharist, though not in the unscriptural and impossible sense of the Romanist. Let there be silence while, as of old, he speaks "peace," while he shows his hands and his feet and his side. It is Christ whom we wish to see and hear. It is with Christ we would renew our covenant. It is from Christ we would receive fresh tokens of love. It is to Christ we would pray.

Many can sympathize with the remark of a pious lady upon a sacramental occasion: "This afternoon Dr. —— dispensed the communion. He told us of many things we ought to pray for at such a time, but he gave us very little time. *I do love a long pause!*"

This also is a reason for silence at the Supper— it is a most fitting time for *prayer*. The believer is communing with his Saviour, and when the Saviour appears in his tenderest compassion. These memorial "elements" attest the great love of Christ for sinners, and furnish the ground of prevailing supplication. Faith is aided by sight; the heart is tender; the worth of the soul is appreciated, as it were in view of the cross. Jesus dies for the lost! Will not Jesus hear prayer for the salvation of the lost? "Hundreds of instances," said a now sainted woman, Mrs. Bethune, "crowd on my remembrance, of answer to prayer put up at the Lord's Table."

Therefore let not the believer be interrupted in

his communion with Christ. At the Lord's Table, shall not the Master be heard rather than his guests?

Though some good things of lower worth
   My heart is called on to resign,
Of all the gifts in heaven and earth,
   The greatest and the best is mine:
The love of God in Christ made known,—
The love that is enough alone,
My Father's love, is all my own.

My soul's Restorer, let me learn
   In that deep love to live and rest,—
Let me the precious thing discern
   Of which I am indeed possessed;
My treasure let me feel and see,
And let my moments, as they flee,
Unfold my endless life in thee.

Let me not dwell so much within
   My bounded heart, with anxious heed,
Where all my searches meet with sin,
   And nothing satisfies my need;—
It shuts me from the sound and sight
Of that pure world of life and light
Which has no breadth or length or height.

Let me thy power, thy beauty see;
  So shall my hopeless labor cease,
And my free heart shall follow thee
  Through paths of everlasting peace.
My strength thy gift, my life thy care,
I shall forget to seek elsewhere
The wealth to which my soul is heir.

I was not called to walk alone,
  To clothe *myself* with love and light;
And for thy glory, not my own,
  My soul is precious in thy sight.
My evil heart can never be
A home, a heritage for me,—
But thou canst make it fit for thee.

A. L. WARING.

PREPARE us, Lord, to view thy cross,
  Who all our griefs have borne;
To look on thee whom we have pierced,—
  To look on thee and mourn.

While thus we mourn, we would rejoice,
  And, as thy cross we see,
Let each exclaim, in faith and hope,
  "The Saviour died for me!"

I asked the heavens, "What foe to God hath done
    This unexampled deed?" The heavens exclaim,
"'Twas man; and we in horror snatched the sun
    From such a spectacle of sin and shame."
I asked the sea: the sea in fury boiled,
    And answered with his voice of storms, "'Twas man;
My waves, in panic at his crime, recoiled,
    Disclosed the abyss, and from the centre ran."
I asked the earth: the earth replied, aghast,
    "'Twas man; and such strange pangs my bosom rent,
That still I groan and shudder at the past."
To man — gay, smiling, thoughtless man — I went,
And asked him next: he turned a scornful eye,
Shook his proud head, and deigned me no reply.

MONTGOMERY.

Wash me anew with each returning day,
Thou sacred, quickening stream of Golgotha;
If unforgiven sin my conscience bear,
Weakness and fear possess me everywhere.
But oh, what beaming life returns once more,
If grace again my wearied soul restore.

'Tis grace that can alone my state improve;
No strength I gain unless forgiving love,
A free and copious stream, shall bear away
My past transgressions from the light of day;
  . For who to meet new strife can armed appear
While foes unconquered linger in the rear?

WHITHER, oh, whither should I fly
  But to my loving Saviour's breast?
Secure within thine arms to lie,
  And safe beneath thy wings to rest.

I have no skill the snare to shun,
  But thou, O Christ, my wisdom art;
I ever into ruin run,
  But thou art greater than my heart.
                              C. WESLEY.

SEE where before the throne he stands,
  And pours the all-prevailing prayer,
Points to his side, and lifts his hands,
  And shows that I am graven there.

He ever lives for me to pray;
  He prays that I with him may reign;
Amen! to what my Lord doth say;
  Jesus, thou canst not pray in vain!
                              C. WESLEY.

CHAPTER XVI.

CHRIST'S OBEDIENCE UNTO DEATH — LESSON OF CONSECRATION — THE MONK — DR. JUDSON — POETRY.

"The servant is not greater than his lord." — John 15 : 20.
"Be thou faithful unto death." — Reb. 2 : 10.

AT the Lord's Table we are taught the lesson of consecration and obedience. Christ, our elder Brother, was "obedient unto death." In this he left us an example, that we should follow his steps. Ere the dawn of creation he said, "Lo, I come: in the volume of the book it is written of me, I delight to do thy will, O my God; yea, thy law is within my heart." At the appointed time having come to earth, this spirit of obedience was manifest in all his words and actions. "My meat is to do the will of Him that sent me, and to finish his work. . . . . I came down from heaven not to do mine own will, but the will of Him that sent me. . . . . I do always those things that please him."

Almost at the end of his earthly course, viewing it as already concluded, he could say, "I have glorified Thee on the earth, I have finished the work which thou gavest me to do."

As we stand at the cross and hear his death-cry, "It is finished," we feel that we witness the conclusion of a *finished life*,—a life perfect in its spirit and its achievements,—which left nothing undone that he came to do,—which, viewed from whatsoever side or in whatsoever part, presents an inimitable example of the "beauty of holiness." His was a consecration most perfect and entire, without a break or a stain; which shrunk from no sacrifice, was appalled by no threats, was deaf to all appeals to the love of ease or wealth or honor, whether the temptation came from earth or from the craft of the adversary; which, when his vows required him to pass into the deep floods of Gethsemane, and the darkness, desertion, and anguish of Calvary, drew not back, but, in the midst of these tremendous trials of his spirit, gave utterance to those sweet, sublime words of submission, "The cup which my Father giveth me, shall I not drink it?"

How powerfully does the inspired exhortation, "Let this mind be in you which was also in Christ Jesus," come home to the Christian heart at the Lord's Table. Here is exhibited his obedience unto death,—the disinterestedness and completeness of his consecration. From this sacred point we look back over the whole life of Him who was cradled in the manger; and, as we trace his footsteps along the pathways of Galilee and Judea as he "went about doing good," and view them at length turned toward the spot at which he had predicted he should die, and there bathed in blood, we are prepared to feel the force of his words to his disciples, uttered near the end of his own earthly work, "As my Father hath sent me, *even so send I you.*" We see what that mission involved on the part of *Christ;* and, in that light, what *his followers* must expect in the fulfilment of *their mission.* The whole heart and the whole life are to be given to their work, for it is the work of Christ, the work which he instituted and illustrated, and which he has committed to his disciples as one with him in spiritual sympathy, as the members of his body to execute his will and carry out the great plan of redemption. Their enlistment is for a life-long service. They are to be faithful unto death, never laying aside the implements of toil for any selfish consideration, in response to any pressing call of business or pleasure, but ever hearing the Master's voice, Follow me, and making all worldly pursuits subsidiary to the interests of that kingdom which shall endure forever. If we are Christ's true disciples, we must follow him in toil, in trial, in suffering, in self-denial, in cross-bearing, and, if need be, even in crucifixion. There is no point at which we may draw back. The servant is not to be above his Master. Obedient unto death is the condition of enlistment and reward. The kingdom of heaven is not for him who, "having put his hand to the plough, looks back." The crown is not for his head who wearies of the race, nor the palms of victory for the hands that "hang down" and cease from labor. The beatific vision of "the King in his beauty" is only for those who watch for his coming, in patient, willing toil, or, if toil is forbidden, who stand and wait in meek submission.

At the memorial hour, when we celebrate an obedience which was inspired by perfect love, and which was unto death, it becomes us to examine our lives in the light of this great example. Have they illustrated the spirit of an indwelling Christ? Professing to have been buried with Christ in baptism,— even baptized into his death,— has our subsequent career been inspired by sincere and earnest endeavors after fellowship with Christ and an imitation of his life? Or have we fainted by the way and turned back? Has the road seemed too toilsome, the cross too heavy, the sacrifice too exacting, the demands of Christ exorbitant, or inconsistent with what we deemed our duty aside from his cause? Have we prayed to be excused from service? Have we sought to satisfy conscience with a partial performance, with a commutation of sacrifice for obedience? Have we consulted our convenience, our selfish preferences, our pride? Have we labored as the hireling, who desires the shadow, or as goaded by conscience and *fearing* to abandon our task, rather than loving it for the Master's sake? While our hands may have labored, has the heart been cold and wandering?

Or, on the other hand, have we honestly aimed, though amid many deeply-regretted imperfections, to do the will of Him who sent us into his vineyard? Have we sought to cultivate it according to the Master's pleasure, and for the maturing of fruit which should be to his glory? Has his will been our law?

In the spirit of unreserved, unselfish obedience, that he might finish the work given him to do, Jesus was ready to endure even the *hidings of his Father's face*. Have we been willing to subordinate our much-prized religious privileges and enjoyments to the performance of duty,—perhaps of uncongenial duty?

"A holy monk of old was surprised one day, — such is the legend, — during his hour of secret prayer, by the personal appearance of the Lord Jesus in his cell. Filled with rapture at the gracious condescension, his whole soul overflowed in love and gratitude, and he exclaimed, 'Here let me breathe out my life; let me die at thy feet, if only I may continue to behold thy gracious countenance, my Lord and my God!'

"At that moment a convent-bell broke rudely in upon his trance of worship, summoning him to the routine of daily duty. Must he go? Was there not sufficient excuse for one day's absence from his post? No. Those clear yet loving eyes that penetrated the depths of his soul and beheld the secret inquiry, offered no encouragement to prolonging happiness at the expense of fidelity.

They seemed rather to say, 'Now the labor, the self-denial; hereafter the glory, the reward.'

"With tearful eyes and slow, reluctant steps, the monk withdrew, casting a last look upon the heavenly vision. Longer than ever seemed the hours of dull observances, and often the question forced itself upon him, '*Is* this the way of holiness? Surely it is bearing the cross, but is it following the Master?' And as often spake the answer of faith in his inmost heart, 'The duty now, the joy hereafter.'

"At length the morning's task was ended, and, with beating heart, the monk hastened to his desolate cell. Lo! it was brighter than ever with the pure radiance of that countenance which is altogether lovely. Words of gracious approval rewarded his self-denial, and the joy of that hour shed its light on all the remaining steps of his lonely pathway."

Our Master calls us not to a "routine of dry and useless observances," but always to a service that is noble and useful. And yet it sometimes demands great self-sacrifice; it breaks in upon our hours of calm meditation and prayer; it leads us into paths which we should not choose, for which we seem to ourselves to be peculiarly unfitted, and from which all our tastes and habits would shrink, and in which, for the time, we experience little else than anxiety and fear.

It was a lonely, desolate path which led through Calvary, through the valley of the shadow of death. Yet Jesus trod it, for it was the path of obedience. What was mere joy compared with duty? "For the joy that was *set before him*, Jesus endured the cross." He was willing to wait. Are we willing to wait the Master's pleasure, at whatever present cost of happiness, even to that degree of self-abnegation which is most trying to the heart that longs for the Saviour's smile, — to work under a cloud?

And yet how true do we often find it, when we yield ourselves up to the call of duty that involves peculiar self-sacrifice and suffering and inconvenience, that

> "All unseen the Master walketh
> By the toiling servant's side."

We feel conscious of a strong arm upholding us, of an inward power, mightier than our own weak, trembling spirit, constraining us forward. We feel an assurance that a joy is *set before us*, even as before Christ, and we press on through the gloom and over the hard road.

The Scripture tells us that "even Christ *pleased not himself*." He who had an unrestricted choice chose *not to please himself*. He was perfectly disinterested and self-sacrificing. "The sorrow which he felt was not on account of his own privations and injuries, but zeal for God's service consumed him, and it was the dishonor cast on God that broke his heart."[1]

In this respect Christ was our pattern. As he, in accomplishing his work, pleased not himself, so we should lay aside all personal considerations and aim ever to please Christ.

Dr. Judson, a man faithful unto death, was once asked whether *faith* or *love* influenced him most in going to the heathen. "I thought of it a while," he said, "and at length concluded that there was in me but little of either. But in thinking of what *did* influence me, I remembered a time, out in the woods back of Andover Seminary, when I was almost disheartened. Everything looked dark. No one had gone out from this country. The way was not open. The field was far distant and in an unhealthy climate. I knew not what to do. All at once that 'last command' seemed to come to my heart directly from heaven. I could doubt

[1] Hodge. *Com. on Romans*.

no longer, but determined on the spot to obey it at all hazards, for the sake of *pleasing the Lord Jesus Christ.*"

In reviewing our lives as it were in sight of the cross, do we feel that the controlling motive has been to please the Lord Jesus, to do the will of him who sent us into his vineyard? Do we find ourselves more and more inclined to follow Christ whithersoever he leads? Does our conscience respond to the reasonableness of an entire consecration to Christ? and does our heart plead for a larger measure of his Spirit to render our obedience more cheerful and perfect?

At the Lord's Table, where our Master shows himself in the perfection of a finished work, we are summoned to meet these questions.

If saddened and disheartened by the retrospect, let the beholding of the symbols of our dear Lord's obedience unto death incite us to new ardor in our course. And let us not only be incited by that great example to quicken our pace and redouble our diligence and bear our cross with more patience, but be led to seek a fresh application to our souls of that precious blood of Christ, which, while it attested his fidelity to the Father's will, also has sovereign power to cleanse from the guilt of our past neglects and shortcomings, and thus to impart anew the spirit of adoption, which is the spirit of love and loyalty. The child of God is the servant of Christ.

Tossed with rough winds and faint with fear,
Above the tempest, soft and clear,
What still, small accents greet mine ear?
  'Tis I; be not afraid.

'Tis I, who washed thy spirit white;
'Tis I, who gave thy blind eyes sight;
'Tis I, thy Lord, thy life, thy light; —
  'Tis I; be not afraid.

These raging winds, this surging sea,
Bear not a breath of wrath to thee;
That storm has all been spent on me; —
  'Tis I; be not afraid.

This bitter cup, — I drank it first;
To thee it is no draught accurst;
The hand that gives it thee is pierced; —
  'Tis I; be not afraid.

Mine eyes are watching by thy bed,
Mine arms are underneath thy head,
My blessing is around thee shed; —
      'Tis I; be not afraid.

When, on the other side, thy feet
Shall rest, 'mid thousand welcomes sweet,
One well-known voice thy heart shall greet;
      'Tis I; be not afraid.

From out the dazzling majesty,
Gently He'll lay his hand on thee,
Whispering, "Beloved, lov'st thou me?
'Twas not in vain I died for thee;
      'Tis I; be not afraid."

So fair a face bedewed with tears!
What beauty e'en in grief appears!
He wept, he bled, he died for you;
What more, ye saints, could Jesus do?

What pity dwelt within his breast!
Pity by flowing tears expressed;
Oh, may those tears our griefs remove,
Which speak so loud a Saviour's love.

THE MEMORIAL HOUR.

I LOVE to kiss each print where thou
  Hast set thine unseen feet;
I cannot fear thee, blessed Will!
  Thine empire is so sweet.
                    FABER.

How blessed, from the bonds of sin
  And earthly fetters free,
In singleness of heart and aim,
  Thy servant, Lord, to be!
The hardest toil to undertake
  With joy at thy command;
The meanest office to receive
  With meekness at thy hand;

With willing heart and longing eyes
  To watch before thy gate,
Ready to run the weary race,
  To bear the heavy weight;
No voice of thunder to expect,
  But follow calm and still,
For love can easily divine
  The one Beloved's will.

Thus may I serve thee, gracious Lord!
  Thus ever thine alone,
My soul and body given to thee,
  The purchase thou hast won;

Through evil or through good report
  Still keeping by thy side;
By life or death, in this poor flesh,
  Let Christ be magnified!

How happily the working days
  In this dear service fly!
How rapidly the closing hour—
  The time of rest—draws nigh,
When all the faithful gather home,
  A joyful company!
And everywhere the Master is
  Shall his blest servants be.

From the German. SPITTA.

CHAPTER XVII.

CHRISTIAN BENEVOLENCE — THE WORK OF THE CHURCH — NATURAL PHILANTHROPY — THE DEATH OF CHRIST AN ELEMENT OF POWER — DUTY TO THE OPPRESSED — POETRY.

"Who went about doing good." — Acts 10 : 38.

VAST is the work of Christian benevolence which lies before the church, — the temporal and spiritual amelioration of mankind. Well does it deserve the deepest thought, the most fervent prayers, and the most abundant toil of every child of God and every lover of his race. With every year there comes a louder call from the whitening harvests.

Abroad, the few laborers faint beneath their burdens even while rejoicing in their sacrifices and successes, and send back the cry, "Come over and help us." At home, the poor and suffering and degraded and benighted still abound. The swelling tide of emigration is bearing to our shores, with many who are enlightened and Christian, multitudes of the superstitious, ignorant, and vicious. The impenitent and Christless are on every side. And at this eventful hour, the millions who are coming forth of their house of bondage present a spectacle of thrilling interest. Was there ever laid upon the Christian conscience and heart so precious and fearful a burden?

Surely there is needed a spirit of broad and hearty benevolence to uplift the weak and oppressed, to instruct the ignorant, to reclaim the degraded, to care for the suffering, to seek and save the perishing.

How shall it be attained? Whence shall it come?

"Our cold and decaying humanity must be fed by a fuller life than its own, must be nourished in a warmer bosom, before it can attain to any enduring heat of nobleness or love."[1]

Whose is that "warmer bosom," that "fuller life"? There can be but one answer. It is that most unselfish, loving, tender, and sinless heart of the Son of God who was also the Son of man. He was anointed to "preach the gospel to the

[1] Dora Greenwell. *Patience of Hope.*

poor, to heal the broken-hearted, to preach deliverance to the captives, and recovering of sight to the blind, to set at liberty them that are bruised, to preach the acceptable year of the Lord." He "went about doing good." His was the heart that yearned with an infinite tenderness over human guilt and grief, that carried our sorrows, and was broken for our offences. The church needs to be warmed into new life by a closer fellowship with that sacred, bleeding Heart, that throbbing Bosom.

In Christ crucified, humanity, wounded and scarred and blasted, has its true Friend, faithful to rebuke, able to heal. At the cross only can be learned the priceless value of the soul,[1] the ruinous

---

[1] "One recalls the sublime rapture of Pascal, the living memory of which he always cherished by carrying about with him a written paper, opening with these words, the broken but glorious expression of a faith unspeakable:—

> 'God of Abraham, God of Isaac, God of Jacob!
> Not the god of the philosophers and wise men;
> Certainty, certainty, love, joy, peace;
> God of Jesus Christ.'

Then comes this significant expression:—

> 'Greatness of the human soul.'

Thus, at the very moment when this great genius throws himself at the feet of Christ, exclaiming, 'Jesus Christ! Jesus Christ! I have cast myself off from him; I have forsaken him, denied, crucified him;

and defiling nature of sin, the beauty of holiness, the majesty of justice, and the true quality of love. To the philanthropy learned of Christ, especially at his cross, there is a breadth and tenderness which the philanthropy springing from the mere natural sensibilities must ever lack. It is more delicate in its instincts, more catholic in its aims. It is the philanthropy of heaven. It is Christ going about " doing good," in the persons of his faithful followers. Such philanthropy forms the truest judgment of what is essential and what only accidental, so that it lays the broadest and surest foundation of reform and culture. Making foremost and vital the spiritual and eternal, it provides also and more effectually for the temporal and earthly. Thus has it lifted up the Sandwich Islanders and the Karens.

The natural impulses of benevolence are often beautiful and effective to a certain point, but they are apt to act blindly and rashly, to run into vague

---

oh, that I may never be severed from him!'—at this moment of 'complete and sweet self-renunciation,' in the dust where he falls, he has the lively consciousness of the greatness of the human soul. And he is not mistaken, for never does it appear greater than in the presence of the Redeemer sacrificed for it. It is at the foot of the cross that one can exclaim, ' The greatness of the human soul!'"— *From the French of Edmond de Pressensé. Critical Review of Renan's Life of Christ.*

and impossible experiments, to stop short of that which should ever form the ultimate end, and to be disheartened by want of visible success.

It is only the benevolence which flows from the union of the heart with Christ that acts wisely, meekly, steadily, untiringly, for the noblest ends, by the surest methods. Following Christ, it cannot go amiss, and it cannot draw back. Then the fountain, which would else run dry or swell into a torrent, replenished from the bosom of infinite Love and Truth, sends forth streams which make glad the desolate places, flowing on and ever.

As Christ shall "not fail nor be discouraged till he have set judgment in the earth," so also they who are one with Christ in spirit and work may sustain their hearts, amid all outward discouragements and adversities, by the consciousness of his living Presence, and by the sure promise that to him shall be given "the heathen for his inheritance, and the uttermost parts of the earth for a possession." If they obey and please Christ, the result and the success may be left with him.

The love of Christ is the inspiration and support of true benevolence, which clings to a Personal Object, to please whom may well satisfy the noblest ambition of the soul. In this respect, Christian philanthropy differs essentially from the benevolence of the natural man.

This must be solid truth, and not mere fancy, unless indeed with the Saviour's ascent from Olivet his Spirit also departed. If his Spirit be a living force, his gospel the power of God, if Christ himself be an actual presence in the world, " the life of men," then must we find in Christ, and only in him, the philanthropy that is to elevate and save mankind. What is needed is a more complete appropriation by the church, by individual disciples, of this celestial benevolence.

The life and death of Christ formed a mighty era, and constitute a mighty element, in human affairs. With reference to man's earthly wellbeing, they have rendered obsolete the old civilizations; they have introduced a new one, which builds upon a foundation as broad and deep as the wisdom and love of God, and which comprehends both worlds. Christian civilization is not content with physical and intellectual culture, with social improvement, with refinement of manners, with civil freedom, with " liberty, equality, and fraternity," though it fosters all these. It first of all exhibits Christ as the Saviour and Model of humanity, who, by revealing the soul to itself, in its sins and miseries and yet vast capacities, and then by revealing himself to that soul as its Redeemer and Brother, can satisfy its deepest wants, awaken its noblest aspirations, and put it in the path of endless progression.

The incarnation and death of Christ bear the most wonderful testimony to the essential equality of men.[1] All are on the same sad level of sin and misery, as needing alike for their salvation the shedding of Christ's precious blood, and yet, as a consequence, on the same plane also of exalted dignity, in that so great a Being assumed their common nature, and suffered in it for their redemption. The lowest in the social scale has "a Brother in the eternal Son of God!" What are all earthly distinctions before such a fact? Well does the Scripture say, "Honor all men." An awful sacredness invests the humblest disciple, a sweet glory attaches to the humblest service done to a disciple in the name of a disciple. In the poor and wretched of Christ's flock we see his own representatives. Christ suffers, Christ is relieved

---

[1] "She [the church] views man not simply as man, but as the image of the God whom she adores. She feels for every one of the race a holy respect, which imparts to him, in her eyes, a venerable character, as redeemed by an infinite price, to be made the temple of the living God."— *Pascal, Provincial Letters,* Let. XIV.

in the persons of his brethren: "Inasmuch as ye have done it unto one of the least of these my brethren, ye have done it unto ME."

In this view, how great the guilt of oppressing God's poor. A distinguished jurist of our country has nobly said, " The sweat-blood which this nation is now shedding at every pore is the awful warning of how fearful a thing it is to oppress the humblest being."[1] What shall we say when in this humble being we recognize the Lord Jesus, and when we consider that for the redemption of this "little one" the sweat-blood of the garden and the life-blood of the cross was shed?

It becomes us to feel that in these long-abused people of a darker hue, many of them his own spiritual brethren, Jesus himself looks to us, pleadingly for sympathy and succor. It is his body that is fettered and lashed, his soul that is wronged and agonized; it is he that is bought and sold; it is he that is accounted as no man, but merchandise,— a thing, "with no rights to be respected;" and therefore it is he, the suffering, sorrowing, lacerated Jesus, that appears before us, holding up his manacled hands and appealing to our Christian hearts.

By our love to the Lord Jesus, by the pity and

---

[1] Judge Dickson, of Cincinnati.

anguish of his soul for us, by our own hope of mercy, let us show mercy to Christ's pleading poor. Let us take them by the hand, and deal tenderly, magnanimously by them, as those whom we have long neglected through selfishness or fear. They look to us for sympathy, protection, guidance, intellectual light, and especially for a pure and unfettered gospel.

As we meet to remember Jesus at his Table, let us open our hearts to the woes and wants of that humanity whose nature he wore, and in which and for which he suffered.

Too little faith has the church had in the power of the gospel, in the promises of God, in the presence of Christ. Too often, in the support of her enterprises of benevolence, have appeals been made to selfish and sordid motives, as if the kingdom of Christ could be built up in the world, and mankind blessed and saved, by resorting to principles and practices foreign to the nature of that pure and holy kingdom; as if Christ, the King in Zion, were unequal to his own work and must borrow weapons from his foes.

Come, then, O Church of Christ, to the Broken Heart, the Wounded Side, to the Son of man, our

Brother yet our Redeemer and Lord, who has all power in heaven and earth; come, and from his unfailing love replenish your hearts. His resources have not been exhausted. He is "the same yesterday, to-day, and forever." However much the church has witnessed of his power in her palmiest days, his fulness is still the same, his gospel as fresh, as vigorous, as full-armed as ever. Never shall the light of the cross pale before the splendors of any new dispensation, but, one by one, all other lights shall be extinguished, and Jesus shall rule, the sole "King of day."

It is for the church to accept the sure word of prophecy touching the Messiah's kingdom, and in the might of a simple and therefore overcoming faith to enter with new energy upon her appointed work.

O Lord Jesus, may the sight of the broken bread and poured-out wine awaken in my heart an intenser love to thee and a more earnest desire to imitate thy heavenly compassion! May my heart become more tenderly responsive to the appeals of a sinning, suffering world! May I behold thee in thine afflicted disciples, and for thy sake hasten to their relief. And may thine approving smile be deemed a rich reward for even the greatest self-denial.

Lord Jesus, forgive my past selfishness, and conform me to thy blessed image.

BRETHREN, go forth beside all ways,
    The wanderer greet with outstretched hand,
And call him back who darkly strays,
    And bid him join our gladsome band.
That Heaven has stooped to earth below,
    Proclaim the glad news everywhere,
That all may learn our faith, and know
    They too may find an entrance there.
              Lyra Germanica.

A POOR wayfaring man of grief
    Hath often crossed me on my way,
Who sued so humbly for relief
    That I could never answer, "Nay."
I had not power to ask his name,
Whither he went or whence he came,
Yet there was something in his eye
That won my love, I knew not why.

Once when my scanty meal was spread,
   He entered,—not a word he spake,—
Just perishing for want of bread;
   I gave him all; he blessed it, brake,
And ate,—but gave me part again;
Mine was an angel's portion then,
For while I fed with eager haste,
That crust was manna to my taste.

I spied him where a fountain burst
   Clear from the rock; his strength was gone;
The heedless water mocked his thirst,
   He heard it, saw it hurrying on;
I ran to raise the sufferer up;
Thrice from the stream he drained my cup,
Dipt, and returned it running o'er;
I drank, and never thirsted more.

'Twas night: the floods were out; it blew
   A winter hurricane aloof;
I heard his voice abroad, and flew
   To bid him welcome to my roof;
I warmed, I clothed, I cheered my guest,
Laid him on my own couch to rest;
Then made the hearth my bed, and seemed
In Eden's garden while I dreamed.

Stript, wounded, beaten, nigh to death,
   I found him by the highway-side;
I roused his pulse, brought back his breath,
   Revived his spirit, and supplied

Wine, oil, refreshment: he was healed;
I had myself a wound concealed,
But from that hour forgot the smart,
And peace bound up my broken heart.

In prison I saw him next, condemned
  To meet a traitor's doom at morn;
The tide of lying tongues I stemmed,
  And honored him 'midst shame and scorn.
My friendship's utmost zeal to try,
He asked if I for him would die;
The flesh was weak, my blood ran chill,
But the free spirit cried, "I will."

Then in a moment to my view
  The stranger darted from disguise;
The tokens in his hands I knew,—
  My SAVIOUR stood before mine eyes;
He spake, and my poor name he named:
" Of me thou hast not been ashamed;
These deeds shall thy memorial be;
Fear not, thou didst them unto me."

JAMES MONTGOMERY.

BE strong, my soul, although to-morrow
  Each earthly joy were from thee torn;
Have courage, though the bitterest sorrow
  Should leave thee comfortless to mourn.

Upraise thee, groveller, from the dust,
In soul to grasp thy God, and trust;
  Be worthy of the glorious lot
Which he who died for thee, the Son,
Has for thee from the Father won.
  This life's a dream that lingereth not.
Striv'st thou with zeal to bless thy kind,
  Still on thy country's good intent?
Were the whole world against thee joined,
  Ne'er of thy righteous zeal repent.
Let neither wile nor mock of sin
Stifle the still small voice within,
Nor hinder thee from deeds of love;
Thy heaven is in the realms above.

I JOURNEY forth rejoicing
  From this dark vale of tears,
To heavenly joy and freedom,
  From earthly bonds and fears,
Where Christ, our Lord, shall gather
  All his redeemed again,
His kingdom to inherit;
    Good-night till then.

I go to see His glory,
  Whom we have loved below;
I go, the blessed angels,
  The holy saints, to know;

Our lovely ones departed
　I go to find again,
And wait for you to join us;
　Good-night till then.

I hear the Saviour calling;
　The joyful hour has come;
The angel guards are ready
　To guide me to our home,
Where Christ, our Lord, shall gather
　All his redeemed again,
His kingdom to inherit;
　Good-night till then.

From the German.

CHAPTER XVIII.

A SUMMARY — REMEMBER CHRIST — THE RELATION OF CHRISTIANITY, IN ITS PERSONAL CHRIST, TO ALL THE CIRCUMSTANCES AND CONDITIONS OF LIFE — ITS TEMPORAL AND ETERNAL BENEFITS — CHRIST EVERYWHERE — POETRY.

"*Ye are complete in Him.*" — *Col.* 2:10.

THE most obvious as it is the most important light in which Christ is to be viewed is that of a Saviour. His name is Jesus, which is Saviour. He came to save us from the wrath to come, to save his people from their sins. This was the grand, crowning object of his mission. Hence the Supper is especially to remind us that we have "redemption through his blood." Whatsoever else we remember or forget, we should not fail to "keep in memory . . . . that Christ died for our sins, according to the Scriptures."

Around this central fact cluster a multitude of others, showing how wide is the sweep of the

Redeemer's incarnation, how it branches out in innumerable ways, how it connects itself with our entire earthly life; so that to remember Christ is to range over a vast field. Indeed, a work so profound as that of Christ in dying for our sins, affecting us as it does at the most vital points, involving so momentous a change in our character and relations, introducing so new and so powerful a principle of action into the sphere of human existence, cannot but have its important bearings on all the phases of our earthly life. It addresses itself to every faculty of man, and gives laws for its exercise.

We have sins to be forgiven, guilt to be washed away, and justification to be secured; with reference to these fundamental points we must remember Christ. We have also earthly relations to sustain, duties to perform, a practical piety to cultivate, a conflict to maintain, temptations to meet, trials to endure, and a perfect holiness to strive for. Here we must remember Christ. In running the race set before us, we must "look unto Jesus;" in waging the Christian warfare, we must follow and trust in the Captain of salvation, "enduring hardness, as good soldiers of Jesus Christ;" in the discharge of duty, we must recognize Christ as our Master, Teacher, Pattern, and Helper; in the midst of trial, the power which shall console us, and which shall convert our sorrows into a heavenly discipline, and thus dignify them into witnesses for God and the gospel of his grace, must come from the remembrance of the "Man of sorrows," our "compassionate High Priest;" in our efforts to advance in the divine life, in holiness, we must feel that "faith is our victory,"— faith in the Son of God, our Redeemer.

There is indeed no situation, whether involving work or joy or trial, in which the presence of Christ is not indispensable to make duty a delight and a success, to heighten and chasten our joys, and lessen and hallow our griefs. In fine, "the life we now live in the flesh, we must live by the faith of the Son of God," by a remembrance of and reliance upon Christ.

Remember me, Christ would say to us, as dying for your sins, as your Example, Guide, and Friend; as now and forever living, your Lord and Master and Intercessor, your "Wisdom, Righteousness, Sanctification, and Redemption." And Christ would teach us to look beyond our personal relations to him, and to view him in all his wide connections with the race, thus indicating the duty of his disciples to spread his knowledge among men, with reference to salvation and all the lawful pursuits of life.

Remember me as the Being in whom all hearts should centre, to whom all affections should cling, on whom all weakness should lean, to whom all sin should be confessed and from whom all pardon sought; for whose glory all plans should be laid and all works performed; the substance of all hopes, the end of all desires, the consummation of all purposes, the answer of all prayers, the solution of all doubts, the key to all the enigmas of Providence, the harmony of life's contradictions and discords, the satisfaction and fulness of all love; the joy of earth, the light and glory of heaven; "by whom and for whom all things were created." Remember me as the guide of childhood, the energy of manhood, the solace of age.

Remember me as the end and sum of science,[1]

---

[1] "Ritter — the most eminent geographer in the world — carried his religion into his scientific studies. . . . . The globe was to him but the place where God's kingdom should be founded; and in all his study of man, Christ became the middle point. In his most valuable scientific writings, the thought that underlies them all — whether his subject be mountain heights or dark valleys, heaths or cities — is, that everything in the world comes from the counsels of God, and has a relation to the kingdom of Christ. . . . . His great aim was to show the workings of the living God in the conditions of history. . . . .

the beauty and highest inspiration of art,[1] the in-

In sending me a copy of his last volume, he wrote in it with his own hand, that it was another note added to the harmony of that general song of praise in which all branches of science must unite, if they will retain the honor which God has lent to them, until the time shall come when they shall raise the 'gloria in excelsis' in still nobler notes."— *Geographical Studies, by Carl Ritter, translated by W. L. Gage.*

"Christ is the Sun of Righteousness, ... and no region in all the circuit of the world's history, or science, or art, is 'hid from the heat thereof,' or fails to supply, when properly scanned, its traces of that Saviour's gracious and glorious rule. . . . . The Christ who is the core of all theology, will, to a mind schooled in God's oracles and under the lessons of the Holy Ghost, be found underlying not only the whole stream of Science as well as History, but also the whole current of Art and Poetry. As 'without him was not anything made that was made,' the microscopic plumage of a moth's wing is to be recognized as his handiwork; and the hues that flush a summer sunset are to be regarded as the exquisite choice of our elder and redeeming Brother."— *William R. Williams, D. D., in the New York Examiner, May* 10, 1860.

[1] Ruskin, in speaking of Turner, the great English painter, gives also the true aim of every artist: " He stands upon an eminence from which he looks back over the universe of God and forward over the generations of men. Let every work of his hand be a history of the one and a lesson to the other. Let each exertion of his mighty hand be both hymn and prophecy,— adoration to the Deity, revelation to mankind." — *Modern Painters*, Vol. I., p. 422.

In comparing the two orders of art, — the classic or Grecian and the Christian, — the same author says, " [They] have in them nothing common; and the field of sacred history, the intent and scope of Christian feeling, are too wide and exalted to admit of the juxtaposition of any other sphere or order of conception; they embrace all other fields like the dome of heaven."— *Modern Painters*, Vol. II., p. 218.

"The image which the brutal insolence of soldiers, as if by the sport of accident, here creates [John 19: 1–6], has become the most touching

terpreter of nature,[1] the conservator of literature, the philosophy[2] of life and being, the spirit of all

representation of divine majesty in the form of a servant, and consequently also the sublimest object of Christian art! How great would have been the loss to our race had they been deprived of this image of majesty in its voluntary humiliation! How calmly yet mightily has it preached through all time, in palace, cottage and cell!"— *Tholuck, Com. on John,* p. 390.

"Culture is far more comprehensive, more varied, more profound [in Christendom than in pagan Greece]; for it is not only affluent with the wealth of days gone by, but Christianity has placed it on the solid foundation of truth."— *Guyot, Earth and Man.*

[1] "There is one other characteristic of Christ to be classed exclusively neither with the intellectual nor the moral powers, but tempering and beautifying both, — his habit of dwelling affectionately on the aspects of nature. . . . . It testifies to an openness to gentle, unexciting influences, to a freshness of soul rejoicing in nature's dewdrops, to an innocence which can sympathize with the tender harmony of nature's joy. It evinces a delicacy of soul that would recoil with sensitive pain from guile, from malignity, from baseness. . . . . In its noble form, this love of nature is eminently a trait of Christian times. . . . . 'I do not know,' says Mr. Ruskin, 'that of the expressions of affection towards external nature to be found among heathen writers, there are any of which the leading thought leans not towards the sensual parts of her. Her beneficence they sought, and her power they shunned; her teaching through both they understood never.' . . . . Now the Person who introduced this finer influence into life, this gentler music into civilization, was Jesus Christ. . . . Christ exalted our whole conception of nature by habitually associating it with the spiritual instruction of man."— *Bayne, The Testimony of Christ to Christianity,* p. 131.

[2] "A sound philosophy comes to this conclusion, — that Christianity fulfills every condition, — that in its God and its incarnate Jesus, its revelation and its atonement, its sanctifying agency and its future heaven, — it responds to every want and hope of humanity."— *Eadie, Com. on Colossians.*

true reform, the hope of humanity, the bond of families,[1] the "Desire of nations," the unity and perfection of the church.

Remember me in every sphere of life, and in all its changeful aspects, — in its days of sunlight or of cloud, of active business or of rest; in the time of peace and the time of war; amid national prosperity or adversity; when the church walks as queen, or when her glory is obscured, and she sits in sackcloth; when converts are as drops of dew, or when hearts are hardened and the godly mourn. Christ is to be remembered as the object of all praise, the source of all joy, the succorer in all trouble, the deliverer from all danger; as the being whose hand can disperse all clouds, conquer all opposition, turn all hearts, and change the shadow of death into the brightness of noonday; as the secret of devout lives and triumphant deaths, and the security and substance of an endless life.

Most truly, then, is the communion season a memorial hour, an hour for recalling to mind the relations of the Crucified and Risen and Reigning

---

[1] "He alone setteth the solitary *in families*, by giving, in his own Person, that common centre for hopes, interests, and affections which is the principle of the family — united life." — *The Patience of Hope*, p. 113.

Saviour to ourselves personally and to mankind,— in all our connections with the present and the future, in all our needs, duties, and hopes. Thus recognizing Christ in all things, will our life have a glorious unity, an ennobling purpose, and a blissful end. Thus shall we be fitted to attain the true end of our being; for Christ came to reconstruct our ruined nature, to bring into harmony its discordant elements, to inspire our souls with the purest and loftiest sentiments, to lead us onward in the path of obedience and usefulness, and at length receive us to himself, as having in him our eternal felicity,—"complete" in him.

Here then is the place to remember Christ, in the formation of new resolutions to serve and glorify him in whatsoever sphere. He who thinks of Calvary—of the scenes of the Redeemer's love and sorrow—will not forget the rest. Loving Christ crucified, we shall love Christ, the Son of man, the living and reigning Saviour. We shall follow Christ whithersoever he leads; we shall keep his commandments. The direction of the suffering Saviour—Remember me—will follow us through the week, everywhere our motto, our watchword, our inspiration, lifting even our common duties out of the low sphere of earthliness into the higher plane of Christian work, and ever prompting to earnest efforts bearing directly upon the spiritual kingdom of Christ and the salvation of the objects of his redeeming love.

> "Remember thee, — thy death, thy shame!
> Our sinful hearts to share!
> O memory, leave no other name
> But his recorded there!"

O Jesus, my Saviour, my King, I love thee, I adore thee! Thou hast loved me and given thyself for me; thou hast suffered dreadful pains and agonies of soul and body to gain for me present peace and eternal felicity! Lord Jesus, I cast myself at thy blessed feet, acknowledging the just supremacy of thy sway, and beseeching thee to make my whole life as one act of love and gratitude. In whatsoever worldly calling, may my spirit be wholly Christian, may I aim to please thee, as thy disciple and servant, so that when summoned to give account of my stewardship, I may do it with joy and not with grief.

And in view of the many imperfections of my service, which must then appear, and all the sins of a whole life, may I be found in thee, clinging solely to thy cross, pleading only thy righteousness, and humbly yet confidently looking for a welcome through the infinite merits of thy blood.

Into thy blessed kingdom may I be at last received, pure and holy through the renewing of the Spirit and the all-pervading influence of thine atonement, there, through eternal ages, to bless the " conduct of thy grace," and join in the songs and services which shall be alike delightful as inspired by the love of Christ.

———⸺∘⦂⊙⦂∘⸺———

Not here, not here! not where the sparkling waters
    Fade into mocking sands as we draw near;
Where in the wilderness each footstep falters;—
    "I shall be satisfied,"— but, oh, not here!

Not here, where every dream of bliss deceives us,
    Where the worn spirit never gains its goal;
Where, haunted ever by the thoughts that grieve us,
    Across us floods of bitter memory roll.

There is a land where every pulse is thrilling
    With raptures earth's sojourners may not know,
Where heaven's repose the weary heart is stilling,
    And peacefully life's time-tossed currents flow.

Far out of sight, while yet the flesh enfolds us,
   Lies the fair country where our hearts abide,
And of its bliss is naught more wondrous told us,
   Than these few words, "I shall be satisfied."

Satisfied! satisfied! the spirit's yearning
   For sweet companionship with kindred minds, —
The silent love that here meets no returning, —
   The inspiration which no language finds, —

Shall they be satisfied? the soul's vague longings, —
   The aching void which nothing earthly fills?
Oh, what desires upon my soul are thronging,
   As I look upward to the heavenly hills.

Thither my weak and weary steps are tending;
   Saviour and Lord, with thy frail child abide!
Guide me towards home, where, all my wanderings
      ending,
   I then shall see thee and "be satisfied."

I NEED Thy *presence* every passing hour;
What but thy grace can foil the tempter's power?
Who like thyself my guide and stay can be?
Through clouds and sunshine, oh, abide with me!

I'll fear no foe with thee at hand to bless;
Ills have no weight and tears no bitterness;
Where is death's sting? where, grave, thy victory?
I triumph still if thou abide with me.

Hold thou thy cross before my closing eyes:
Shine through the gloom, and point me to the skies.
Heaven's morning breaks, and earth's vain shadows
    flee!
In life, in death, dear Lord, abide with me.

H. L. LYTE.

WHAT joy, while thus I view the day
That warns my thirsting soul away,
  What transports fill my breast!
For lo! the great Redeemer's power
Unfolds the everlasting door,
  And leads me to his rest.

The festive morn, my God, is come
That calls me to the hallowed dome,
  Thy presence to adore;
My feet the summons shall attend,
With willing feet thy courts ascend,
  And tread the ethereal floor.

E'en now to my expecting eyes
The heaven-built towers of Salem rise;
  E'en now, with glad survey,
I view her mansions that contain
Th' angelic forms, an awful train,
  And shine with cloudless day.

Hither, from earth's remotest bound,
Lo! the redeemed of God ascend,
  Their tribute hither bring;
Here, crowned with everlasting joy,
In hymns of praise their tongues employ,
  And hail the immortal King;—

Great Salem's King, who bids each state
On her decrees dependent wait;
  In her, ere time began,
High on eternal base upreared,
His hands the regal seat prepared
  For Jesse's favored Son.

Let me, blest seat, my name behold
Among thy citizens enrolled,
  In thee forever, dwell;
Let Charity my steps attend,
My sole companion and my friend,
  And Faith and Hope farewell.

From the Latin of Zwinger, by Merrick.

I REST with thee! Eternal life the prize
  Thou wilt bestow, when faith's good fight is won;
What can earth give but vain regrets and sighs,
  To the poor heart whose passing life is done?
For lasting joys I fleeting ones resign,
Since Jesus calls me his, and he is mine.

I rest with Thee! no other place of rest
    Can now attract, no other portion please;
The soul, of heavenly treasure once possessed,
    All earthly glory with indifference sees.
Poor world, farewell! thy splendors tempt no more;
The power of grace I feel, and thine is o'er.

I rest with Thee! with thee, whose wondrous love
    Descends to seek the lost, the fallen raise.
Oh that my whole of future life might prove
    One hallelujah, one glad song of praise!
So shall I sing, as time's last moments flee,
Now and forever, Lord, I rest with thee!

      ADOLPH MORAHT. *Hymns from the Land of Luther.*

CHAPTER XIX.

THE PROPHETIC CHARACTER OF THE SUPPER — CHRIST'S SECOND COMING — HIS PERPETUAL PRESENCE — CONSOLATION TO THE CHURCH — CHRIST'S SECOND ADVENT TOO MUCH OVERLOOKED — POETRY.

"*Even so, come, Lord Jesus.*" — Rev. 22:20.
"*Till He come.*" — 1 Cor. 11:26.

IN the Lord's Supper we discover a reference not only to the past but to the *future*. It is a memorial and a *prophecy*. It commemorates the death of Christ and predicts his second coming. "Ye do show the Lord's death *till he come*."

Christ, then, is risen; he lives; he still retains the deepest affection for his Church, the purchase of his blood; his separation is only for a time; he shall come again. When the purpose of his absence shall have been accomplished, through the dispensation of the Spirit, he shall revisit the scene of his incarnation and suffering, appearing visibly in the air, in the same manner as he had departed.[1]

The Lord's Supper, therefore, directs the gaze of the Church to that amazing event, so interesting in itself and fraught with such momentous consequences to the world. Every new participation is a new act and expression of faith in this promise of Christ, a reiteration of the fact, Christ lives, and of the prophecy, Christ is coming. Age after age shall take up the blessed evangel and bear it onward, till the parting heavens shall give back to earth Him who had moistened it with the blood of his agony; not now a sufferer, but a conqueror and king; not now "to make an offering for sin," but "without sin unto salvation."

The importance of the regular and constant observance of this ordinance is apparent. It is a continuous testimony to Christ as the central Figure of this world's history, not only while he was in the flesh, but through its whole duration; and towards whom, therefore, every eye should be directed with the deepest personal interest. Ere he came to dwell in it and die in it, his coming and dying were predicted as events of the greatest

[1] Acts i. 11.

moment to mankind. May not the "sons of God" have "shouted for joy" at the laying of the earth's corner-stone, specially because they were to sing again over the plains of Bethlehem? While in the flesh, Christ's wide and profound connection with our race was made manifest, and every day is developing its far-reaching influence. When leaving the world, he instituted an ordinance intended to keep in lively remembrance his relation to mankind as its only Helper, and to foretell his second advent in majesty and glory, as still the earth's Lord and the Head of his Church, who would make every knee bow before him, and every tongue confess that he is Lord, to the glory of God the Father. Then it shall be seen how all this world's happiness was wrapped up in Christ, how his smile was life and his frown death.

At the Lord's Table we declare that Christ is "the same yesterday, to-day, and forever;" that we believe his heart is now yearning over his redeemed, as when it was once broken for their offences; that his elect are never for a moment out of mind; and that he is preparing for them a glory which he shall hereafter personally announce and bestow.

Thus Christ fills the entire field of vision. If

we look to the past, what form so conspicuous, so glorious as his? If to the future, all the hopes of the church centre in him.

The Lord's Supper declares that there are no broken links in the chain of Messianic love. The past, the present, the future are one, because Christ at once covers the whole. Nothing is imperfect and fragmentary. The great plan of mercy is complete. Its execution is in the hands of One who cannot "fail nor be discouraged, till he have set judgment in the earth." *Christ shall come,*—therefore all is safe.

In the natural world, the icy fetters of winter may bind the earth, but we know that spring shall come, and with gentle violence undo those fetters; and then it shall be seen that the life of Nature had only slumbered, or been working quietly and unseen, while new beauty shall break forth on every hand. So the church may have its season of winter, of trial and conflict, when her chief memorial is of death,— the death of her beloved Lord. But we know that the "Prince of life" shall come, and then indeed shall " the winter be past, the rain be over and gone, the flowers appear on the earth, the time of the singing of birds have come, and the voice of the turtle be heard in the land." The presence of the Beloved shall make all things new. Death shall now be "swallowed up of life." The long day of glory has come to the church. Her Lord is with her, never more to "go away." Then shall he reveal to her all that, in his absence, he had been doing for her welfare; then shall he celebrate the holy Supper anew in his kingdom, — the marriage-supper of the Lamb, — when he shall present her to himself as his spotless bride.

"Every celebration of the Lord's Supper is a foretaste and prophetic anticipation of the great marriage-supper which is prepared for the Church, at the second appearance of Christ."[1] Then it shall appear how every year of the church's pilgrimage had, under the guidance of the Holy Spirit, the Comforter, been preparing for that great event; how the materials for its august celebration had been gathering amid sorrows, trials, and persecutions, in sympathy with the sufferings of Christ; how the jewels which shall adorn the Bride, the Lamb's wife, had been polishing under the Master's hand.

The continual commemoration of *Christ's suf-*

---

[1] Thiersch.

ferings and death is to perpetually remind his disciples that as He was "made perfect through suffering," so they must be; and that as he passed through it all to "the joy that was set before him," so, at his coming, they are to "enter into the joy of their Lord."

While the church observes this ordinance, she waits in expectation. Upon the eastern sky she fixes her gaze, until the flush of the glad morning shall herald the advent of the Sun of Righteousness; she pitches her tent upon the borders of that ocean which rolls between her and Him whom she longs to see face to face, until he shall come to "dissolve" her "tabernacle" and receive her into the "house not made with hands, eternal in the heavens."

Looking at the promise of Christ to come again, we see a peculiar and touching propriety in its being associated with the memorials of *his death*. Can he leave *her* forever for whom he had poured out his soul unto death? Must he not return, even as the absent husband to his bride, to reassure her of his undying affection, and take her to himself in immortal union? Here is the pledge of his unchangeable love. The Supper, as the memorial of his love in death, proves that though for a season absent in the flesh, he is always present in spirit, and is preparing for her greater glory at the day of the heavenly espousals. "The Supper is the pledge and symbolic seal of Christ's own ever-continued fellowship with his disciples."

What rich consolations for the suffering church flow from this amazing ordinance. She now dwells amid the confusions and conflicts of the world, the endless agitations of society, the seeming triumphs of the wicked, and only half-developed or wholly-mysterious providences. But this sacrament assures her that Christ is to come in person; and then all will be changed. He will dispel all darkness, rectify all disorders, remove all abuses, cast out all things that offend, and conform all things to his perfect law. There shall be "a new heaven and a new earth, wherein dwelleth righteousness."

At present, too, the church is subject to divisions and separations. The Table itself is a place for greetings and farewells. From amid the windings and hardships of her march through the wilderness, dusty and wayworn, and perhaps scarred with "the marks of the Lord Jesus," the sacramental host meets from time to time, each company in its own encampment, to renew its strength in the remembered Christ, and to reaffirm its faith in his coming; but it meets only to separate, each to resume his implement of toil or weapon of warfare. And so, through mingled lights and shades, meetings and partings, the church presses forward to the end.

But the Supper declares that Christ shall come, and then the long-scattered or often-divided flock shall be gathered into the one fold, to be forever with the Lord.

The modern church, even with the constantly renewed testimony of this ordinance, has permitted this great subject to pass too much out of mind; and hence many of the evils which afflict her; hence, in no small measure, her vacillation and timidity.

How different with the ancient Christians. "Their longing desires hastened toward the reappearing of their Lord. It was with them as with the traveller, who beholds from afar the goal of his pilgrimage. His eye embraces at one glance the whole intermediate space; the windings of the intervening way are overlooked, and the distant boundary on which his gaze is fixed seems just at hand."[1] These primitive disciples treasured in their hearts the Redeemer's farewell words, uttered in connection with the last supper: " Let not your heart be troubled; ye believe in God, believe also in me. In my Father's house are many mansions; if it were not so, I would have told you. I go to prepare a place for you. And if I go and prepare a place for you, I will come again and receive you unto myself, that where I am there ye may be also." Blessed words, which cheered the saints of olden time, and which the Supper was intended to keep in glad remembrance.

We who live nearer the great event, should not cease to "look for and haste unto the coming of the day of God." It ill befits *us* to advance with tardy steps, as though uncertainty hung over the future. "Courage, brothers," said the sainted Leighton, "the day is coming!"

Whenever, then, we meet at the Lord's Table, let us look upon it not only as commemorative, but prophetic. We celebrate alike the death of Christ and his kingly triumph. We adore the crucified Redeemer and the reigning Lord. We express our faith in his second coming, and in the

---

[1] Neander. *Com. on* 1 *John.*

glory which shall be revealed in " all them that love his appearing."

> "A little while!" look forward and hope on!
>   Soon shall the troubled dreams of night be gone;
>   The shadows pass away
>   Before the abiding day;
>   The Saviour comes to claim and bless his own.

A CHILD of God! and can this earth's vain pleasures
  Be aught to thee for whom the Saviour died?
Rise, rise above them all!—its worthless treasures,
  Its soul-destroying joys, its pomp and pride;
Be His in all; thy soul and eye be single,
  Fixed as the glory that surrounds the throne;
Seek not Christ's service with the world to mingle,
  Remember, God has sealed thee for his own.

O child of God! be not this earth thy dwelling,
  But stand, in spirit, on that glassy sea
Where the rich harmonies, forever swelling,
  Sound forth the slain Lamb's love, so full, so free;
Stand forth in peace, far above all the madness
  Of sinful man, weighing with even scale
The worth of all things,—feeling the deep gladness
  Of one *who follows Christ within the veil.*

Child of the living God! what boundless blessing!
　His Spirit thine, to comfort and refine;
The heir of God! joint-heir of Christ! possessing
　All things in him, and he himself, too, thine.
Hold fast thy crown, go forth with joy to meet him;
　Soon will he come and take thee for his own;
With girded loins and burning lamps then greet him;
　The bridegroom's triumph thine, thine, too, his throne.

Sweet must it be to dwell secure
From sinful stain, from thought impure,
No wandering footstep to retrace,
No mourning for the Saviour's face;—
And this our happy lot shall be
When we have crossed the crystal sea.

How oft the struggling spirit tries
For blest communion with the skies;
How oft we pray that we may bear
Christ's perfect image even here;
And, oh, like Jesus we shall be
When we have crossed the crystal sea.

They who have safely gone before,
Whose feet grow weary never more,
Receive in that dear land of bliss
All their souls panted for in this;
And their enjoyment ours shall be
When we have crossed the crystal sea.

THE MEMORIAL HOUR.

I see them now in spotless white;
I hear their song of sweet delight;
Beside the living stream they rest,
And Jesus made them truly blest;
With that bright throng we, too, shall be
When we have crossed the crystal sea.

"And so shall we ever be with the Lord."

O SWEET home-echo on the pilgrim's way,
   Thrice welcome message from a land of light!
As through a clouded sky the moonbeams stray,
   So on eternity's deep shrouded night
Streams a mild radiance from that cheering word,
   "So shall we be forever with the Lord."

At home with Jesus! He who went before
   For his own people mansions to prepare;
The soul's deep longing stilled, its conflicts o'er,
   All rest and blessedness with Jesus there.
What home like this can the wide earth afford?
   "So shall we be forever with the Lord."

With him all gathered! to that blessed home
   Through all its windings, still the pathway tends;
While ever and anon bright glimpses come
   Of that fair city where the journey ends, —
Where all of bliss is centred in one word,
   "So shall we be forever with the Lord."

Here, kindred hearts are severed far and wide
  By many a weary mile of land and sea,
Or life's all-varied cares and paths divide;
  But yet a joyful gathering shall be,
The broken links repaired, the lost restored;
  " So shall we be forever with the Lord."

And is there *ever* perfect union here?
  Ah! daily sins lamented and confessed,
They come between us and the friends most dear,
  They mar our blessedness and break our rest. —
With life we leave the evils long deplored:
  " So shall we be forever with the Lord."

Oh, blessed promise! mercifully given!
  Well may it hush the wail of earthly woe;
O'er the dark passage to the gates of heaven
  The light of hope and resurrection throw!
Thanks for the blessed, life-inspiring word, —
  " So shall we be forever with the Lord."
        META HAUSER. *Hymns from the Land of Luther.*

ONE song employs all nations; and all cry,
" Worthy the Lamb, for he was slain for us!"
  The dwellers in the vales and on the rocks
  Shout to each other, and the mountain-tops
  From distant mountains catch the flying joy;
  Till nation after nation taught the strain,

Earth rolls the rapturous hosanna round.
. . . .
Come then, and, added to thy many crowns,
Receive yet one, the crown of all the earth,
THOU who alone art worthy!

COWPER. *Task.*

John 16: 18.

OH for the peace which floweth as a river,
   Making life's desert places bloom and smile!
Oh for the faith to grasp heaven's bright " forever,"
   Amid the shadows of that " little while."

" A little while " for patient vigil-keeping,
   To face the storm, to wrestle with the strong;
" A little while " to sow the seed with weeping,
   Then bind the sheaves and sing the harvest song.

" A little while " to wear the robe of sadness,
   And toil with weary step through miry ways;
Then to pour forth the fragrant oil of gladness,
   And clasp the girdle round the robe of praise.

" A little while," midst shadow and illusion,
   To strive, by faith, love's mysteries to spell;
Then read each dark enigma's bright solution,
   And hail sight's verdict, " He doeth all things well."

"A little while" the earthen pitcher taking
　　To way-side brooks, from far-off fountain fed;
Then the cool lip its thirst forever slaking,
　　Beside the fulness of the fountain-head.

"A little while," to keep the oil from failing,
　　"A little while," faith's flickering lamp to trim;
And then the Bridegroom's coming footsteps hailing,
　　To haste to meet him with the bridal hymn.

www.ingramcontent.com/pod-product-compliance
Lightning Source LLC
Chambersburg PA
CBHW032121230426
43672CB00009B/1813